SMALL TOWN, BIG RESCUE

A Motorcycle Rider's Amazing Story of Rescue, Recovery & Faith in a Colorado Mountain Town

Mike Gallagher

With Andrew Garvey & Glen Sharp

27 Rivers Press
New York - London

DEDICATED TO

MY SAVIORS,

KNOWN AND UNKNOWN

Introduction

Andrew Garvey

Mike Gallagher is the sort of free spirit who called Colorado home before it was cool to live there. He likes the mountain wind on his face and the smell of the aspen trees in his nose. Most of all, he likes the exhilaration of riding a good motorcycle on some good roads.

I first met Mike a few years ago, in 2014, at the dog park in our town of Buena Vista, Colorado. He had his brown Labrador Retriever, Gertie, with him, and I had my Dachshund-Weiner mix, Winthrop, with me. The dogs played great, so we got along fine, too.

He'd always worked jobs like construction and carpentry, but the first thing that struck me about Mike as we sat on the bench under a boxelder maple east of the park, was that he must have been a surfer. He didn't say things like "gnarly" or "hang ten," but it was his bearing that said it for him: tanned and handsome, cool in his Native sunglasses, with his chin at a higher angle than most. It was almost a superior sort of look if you've never met surfers before and don't know how they are. The fact is, surfers tend to look off into the distance – farther than most – for the next big wave to come in and will hold most of a conversation without needing to look at you. It's not arrogance; it's people paying attention to the world coming at them. Mike wasn't a surfer, but as a motorcycle rider, he was always ready for the next drive.

It was in the afternoons that I always saw Mike and Gertie at the dog park. Mike's schedule kept him busy in the mornings. I slowly got to know him over the course of a few months. Our town had a fair population of vacationers passing through, so you never knew if you'd see the same people again. Even most locals' visits to the dog park were spotty, but Mike turned out to be a regular because he loved Gertie and wanted her to enjoy things.

The next summer, in 2015, Mike stopped showing up.

I saw plenty of people at that dog park, and while I noticed he was gone, it didn't seem unusual. The locals tended to be seasonal or somewhat itinerant, and I figured he had taken a trip somewhere interesting to enjoy the numerous sports he and the people of that area participated in. In fact, when I first moved to town, Mike was one of the people who told me about the adventurous nature of the place that had drawn him there. When I asked what to do for fun – and I remember this, specifically, because I repeated it to anyone else who asked – he replied, "There are about forty things to do here. Pick ten."

Hiking, mountain biking, motorcycle riding, four-wheeling, rock climbing, skiing, snowboarding, skijoring (being pulled on skis by a horse over moguls on flat ground), snowshoeing, cross country skiing, snowmobiling, ice fishing, ice climbing, kayaking the Arkansas river, paddle boarding, whitewater rafting, fly fishing, swimming or relaxing in the hot springs, hunting, gold panning, photography, birdwatching, golf, disc golf, foraging for seasonal foods like pine nuts and raspberries, yoga, regular concerts with big name bands, and community dog walks every Saturday were among the most popular things to do. Buena Vista was a dream come true for people who love the out-of-doors.

I didn't think much of Mike's absence until one day an entire year later, in 2016, he showed up at the dog park with a different dog, and Mike was walking with a cane and had only one leg.

"What the hell happened to you, Mike?" I asked, pointing to his leg as we sat down on a bench.

He proceeded to tell me the story about how he wrecked his motorcycle on his favorite ride, going up Cottonwood Pass outside Buena Vista.

He didn't shift correctly on a curve, and launched off the road into a ravine. He was pinned, bleeding, under both a tree and his motorcycle for he didn't know how long.

He tried using his motorcycle key to cut through the tree, making little progress as he passed in and out of consciousness.

Exactly how long Mike was there is uncertain, but a

forensic surgeon estimated it was about 33 hours before a passing bicyclist found him and called for rescue services.

Finally, Mike was saved by what turned out to be the perfect group of professional rescuers with serendipitous timing and the exact equipment needed to save his life.

I was stunned, concerned, and completely fascinated by the story. Every year in Buena Vista and Chaffee County, many people die from far less in pursuit of their adventures. Mike's predicament had certainly been dire. The man had cheated death.

It was an authentic survival story that needed telling.

The next couple of times I saw Mike at the dog park, I urged him to write a book about the experience, but he sort of waved his hand and said he'd never done anything like that before and he didn't know where to start. I gave him several suggestions, but they didn't stick. Almost out of frustration, and certainly because of my love of story, I ordered a digital audio recorder from Amazon and kept it in my vehicle for the next time I saw him.

When I did see him next, he was getting used to walking without the cane and I gave him the recorder in its packaging.

"Just start talking," I said. "Just get some words into that thing and see where it goes."

I explained to him that, as a writer, I was often told by random people, "I've thought about writing a book but never got around to it," or, "I've got a great story for a book; do you want to write it for me?" and how common and irritating that was because I usually never thought their stories sounded very interesting. But, here I was pushing Mike to get something down on record because it was one of the best survival stories I'd ever run across in person.

He relented, accepted the recorder, and began his book with the same focused determination that's helped him in sports and in life. Everyone who knows him knew he'd finish it, because that's how he does things. He may not have been able to saw through that pine tree with his motorcycle key, but he grew this book with the same dedication and willpower.

Throughout his physical recovery, he wondered about who helped him get another chance at life. He had no recollection of the rescue.

Once he regained some mobility, he took his audio recorder and started tracking down everyone he could from the crash scene and hospital to thank them and learn what happened.

It took a group of observant, skilled, and caring passersby and search-and-rescue personnel to save Mike Gallagher.

What he learned on his quest changed him, and maybe it'll change you, too.

Andrew Garvey
is the author of
two books of poetry and coloring art,
The Color of Poetry *and* Quietus,
and a science-fiction novel, Mind Control Empire.

PART ONE:

The Ride and The Crash

Chapter One
The Ride

I'm currently trying to put my mind frame to the day of the accident, back in June 2015. I'm currently driving up from Salida, Colorado. I'm really tired, having been up all night writing. I'm energized by this project but by the same token, slightly ... at this point I think I'm completely overwhelmed, but I must press on.

I'm trying to put myself in the frame of mind I was in at the time.

I love Buena Vista, Colorado, and I love Chaffee County. It's nestled in the Collegiate Peaks region of the Colorado Rocky Mountains, where some of the mountains are named after famous universities. Since the first day I moved here more than a decade ago, I realized just how gorgeous it is here. The color palette changes daily, sometimes by the hour.

At the time I was living in downtown Buena Vista,

renting a house on North Colorado Avenue right across from Alpine Lumber. Everybody knows where Alpine Lumber is.

Gertie and I would walk out my back door, through my backyard, down to the disc golf course then back up through town. For dog owners, and I can only speak for myself, but to have that kind of access to walk your dog a minimum of twice a day is a dream come true. As I would walk up Main Street, I would see the transformation of downtown Buena Vista as it was going through changes from super-small mountain town to a retirement community and action-vacation getaway. It was really neat.

Through it all, I was just the guy who walked the big brown friendly dog.

Unfortunately for me, my beloved dog Gertie, Gertrude, ingested some rat poison and, shortly after, she started going into seizures and becoming disoriented.

My dog was on the path to death, and I still blame myself for her untimely ending. When I took her to be euthanized, it was a moving moment for me. My friend Tom Bell witnessed it. I brought a special Bible and said a special prayer. They stuck the needle in and within seconds she was gone. I said another prayer right after she went, and that was it. Even in death, she did not make a mess out of herself. I wrapped her up in her blanket, and started preparing for a Viking-like funeral pyre for her entry into Valhalla. I took her to a special spot that some of you know where it is. Her funeral lasted about 18 hours and when it was over, there was nothing but fine ashes left behind.

I had a heavy heart and a confused mind. With Gertie gone, what was I going to do? Where should I go?

I know I was in some kind of trance and that trance nearly killed me. It is an understatement to say I had a lot on my mind that day I crashed.

My favorite recreational and emotional outlet was riding my motorcycle up one of the most fantastic driving roads in America. It was just a couple of miles from where I lived.

About six months before Gertie's death, a special motorcycle came into my life, and it proved to be a great stress reliever.

***

Throughout my life, I've ridden motorcycles both street and dirt. I love them! I enjoy riding fast, and I agree with the quote, "When the thrill of speed overcomes all fear of danger, that is the true essence of the addiction to speed."

At the time I owned my first motorcycle I was living in a western suburb of Cleveland, Ohio, called Rocky River. It was where I learned a lot of my bad habits.

My first motorcycle was a 1982 Yamaha Seca 650cc Turbo. The motorcycle was one of the quintessential examples of the 1980s Japanese movement to bring turbo chargers to motorcycles. Interestingly enough, the engine only puts exhaust through one of its dual exhaust pipes. The other was designed for exhaust "over boost" coming through the turbocharger.

A good friend of mine at the time, Alex Rossborough, started working at a local motorcycle dealership, and told me about this great bike they had. It wasn't the first time someone had told me "this is the bike for you" about that specific bike, which I ended up getting.

Not only was the motorcycle fast stock, but they pinned open the wastegate on the turbo and that made the bike incredibly fast. All you had to do was get the motorcycle past 2,500 rpm and the turbo would kick in and instantly put you to the red line. You just started shifting gears as fast as you could, lean forward over the gas tank and hold on. It was all you could do to keep the front tire down on the road.

Rocky River was not known for having "driver's roads." The streets looped around so much that many people called it "Tangle Town." Yet, this made the city the perfect place to learn about speed, cornering and braking – points all essential if you want to ride confidently and fast.

My main hangout back then was Zeke's Bar and Grill in downtown Rocky River. It was a great place to go, and on most nights my friends and I would close the place down at 2:30 a.m. The reason I bring up this fact is that across the street from the bar was a supermarket parking lot where the Rocky River police would wait and watch the comings and goings of Zeke's bar patrons. On many, many occasions, I outran the Rocky River police.

The police would see me out there, and I'd fire up that bike, looking right at them across the street. I'd put my helmet on super tight, step over the bike, and then the race was on!

All I had to do was get them into Tangle Town and the contest was never even close. The amazing fact was they knew who I was, they knew where I lived, and they never, never caught me.

Knowing the area like the back of my hand, I would do giant figure eights on various streets. Police cars, or high-

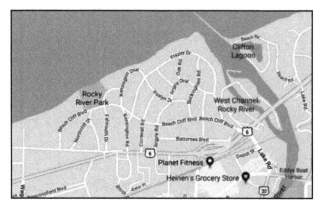

Mike learned to handle curves in the Tangle Town area of Rocky River, Ohio, on the shore of Lake Erie.

performance sports cars for that matter, could not keep up with my motorcycle's ability to corner and accelerate at very high speeds. My final move was to basically cut through my neighbors' backyards and ride right into my backyard. The only problem with that maneuver was I had to turn the bike off; if you did this too fast, the intercooler on the turbo didn't have enough time to cool down. The end result was the turbo would end up cracking. There's always a price to pay when you're having that much fun.

While still in Rocky River, I had my first motorcycle crash. My friend just bought a 1983 Yamaha RD 350. It was a two-stroke, liquid-cooled, 347cc engine equipped with the revolutionary Yamaha power valve system. This was a race bike pure and simple. I remember clearly my friend telling me to wait for it to warm up properly. Well, I got on the bike and on the first turn I made, the bike shot up and through me, tumbling down on to the street. Thank God, I was not physically injured but my pride as a motorcyclist took a real hit. The bike was slightly damaged and I had to buy him a new gas tank. He was a real jerk – he didn't even install the new tank, he used it as a coin jar.

After moving to Marin County, California – San Rafael, to be specific – I purchased a brand new 1987 Honda

Hurricane 600. The original CBR 600 was Honda's first inline, four-cylinder, fully faired sport bike. Mine was white and red. I was afforded access to one of the world's best driving roads, "The Panoramic." It starts out, basically, on Highway 1 in the town of Mill Valley, California, and winds up and over Mount Tamalpais State Park then winds down to Stinson Beach. After a quick break at the beach, it goes onward north through the small surf town of Bolinas, then twists and turns all the way back to San Rafael. It's quite a ride and one I'll never forget.

On one drive, I was traveling on Highway 101 just past Marin City when a softball-sized rock was thrown out by the

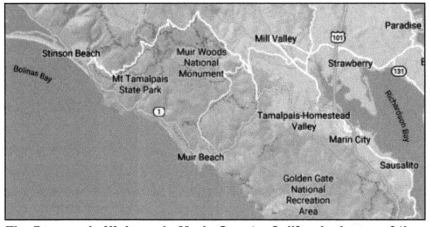

The Panoramic Highway in Marin County, California, is one of the most epic drives in the world.

dual wheels of a dump truck. I saw it coming and I ducked, but the rock hit me in the top of my helmet. The rock shattered my helmet, but if I hadn't been wearing one, I'd have been killed instantly. It was one of many close calls that made me appreciate how fragile life can be.

***

Before Gertie died, I bought a 2006 BMW R 1150 R

Rockster. It has many nicknames such as "The Naked Boxer," because its engine is exposed, and the "Marty Feldman bike," because the one large headlamp and a much smaller headlamp look like the actor who played "Eye-Gore" in the movie *Young Frankenstein*. The engine was technically an Evo-Boxer four-valve, high-cam rocker layout, which has been the backbone of BMW motorcycles for close to 90 years.

Quite frankly, I thought it was slow. It could do a smooth 125 mph, but anything after that was too much for the bike. The fastest I went was 135 mph and the touring bag ripped off. I must have hit some kind of wind shear or something, but I thought it was a blown tire. When it happened, I knew "The Big Guy Upstairs" once again had his hands on that bike and calmed it down because crashing at that speed usually equates to death. I had a badge glued to the fuel tank, a religious icon of the Sacred Heart of Jesus. The words on it read, "I will bless everyplace where a picture of my heart, shall be exposed and honored."

You know, that bike leaked oil like crazy and I could never figure that out. It was a cool bike to have and people went nuts for it for some reason.

***

Cottonwood Pass is probably one of the best driving roads I've ever ridden.

At the top of the pass is the Continental Divide. The summit of Cottonwood Pass is 12,126 feet and has an elevation gain of 4,161 feet from the stoplight in Buena Vista. Cottonwood Pass is what I consider to be a low-level box canyon, a characteristic that is a huge contributing factor to weather and road conditions. This pass is considered extremely dangerous, and has claimed so many lives that authorities have lost count. During all seasons on Cottonwood Pass, you risk death or serious injury from traffic, avalanche, ice, bears, etc. using any form of transport, from walking to snowmobile to car.

There are many factors on Cottonwood Pass that affect driving on any given day. You can't just go up there "Bonsaiing" the pass; it demands your ultimate respect and focus.

Anytime you ride up there, you could expect to deal with moisture on the road – from a wet spot to whole sections layered with frost. Any of these conditions can not only take out motorcycles but even high-performance sports cars.

I am an experienced motorcycle rider and I rode Cottonwood Pass as often as I could, usually solo. Ninety percent of the time I would wear a two-piece KTM riding suit, complete with Kevlar and padding. I also wore motocross boots underneath my pants for added protection. Road racing gloves were a must. These also were padded and had Kevlar plating. Of course I wore a high-end Shoie helmet. I was prepared to ride seriously and ready to encounter any weather or hazardous road conditions.

***

I had a personal code of ethics when I rode Cottonwood Pass, and I want to dispel any ideas that I was out there "dive bombing" everybody and their brothers.

I would be very conscientious when it came to passing vehicles. For example, "mom, pop and the kids" in their Jeep pulling some kind of overweight trailer and taking pictures with their phones, I wouldn't mess with them. But some huge truck, like a Ford F-450, pulling a huge triple-axle toy hauler with an eight-inch exhaust pipe bellowing thick black smoke as it accelerated up the pass – now, those guys want you ripping past and, quite frankly, would be disappointed if you didn't.

If I came up to a line of vehicles, I'd find a place to turn around and hunt for open road. Like with powder skiing or snowboarding, it's a matter of looking for the best conditions.

In town, I always observed the speed limits because I respect the community that I live in. Plus, who needs the stress of being caught when you can just go the speed limit? It's just that simple.

Chapter Two

The Crash

Up to the old stoplight here in Buena Vista. In our town, it's a major waypoint. You can go north, south, east and west on it.

I pull up to the light and I don't mind hitting red. I just let the bike heat up. Like I said, I really respect the speed limits in town.

Buena Vista is a beautiful place. We have a great library, a five-star gold standard in my opinion. I'd see those ladies every day and they saw what was going on with me, cheering me on.

Cruising up here, you have to pay respect to other drivers. If there's an elderly gentleman, you pay respect. There's no reason for me to tailgate the guy like I'm some idiot from Denver trying to get back from City Market grocery avoiding the rush before traffic gets too crazy.

The aspen trees are turning colors as I write this. This year, it's actually pretty cool for me personally because the last two years I've missed Fall due to being hospitalized.

Cottonwood Pass is absolutely gorgeous. Right off on the left is epic Mount Princeton. I think it stands 14,192 feet high. Spread before it, the beautiful aspen groves are all turning yellow and burnt orange.

As I drove west that day – June 7, 8 or 9 of 2015 (the lack of certainty will be made clear) – I got my bike warmed up, trying to get a read on the traffic, it's just a lot of trying to get heat in the tires and getting ready to go. I took this ride very seriously. There were definitely situations where I could really make time up this road. It's just an extremely fun ride.

People who are mesmerized by the speed and the thrill of motorcycle riding can understand. Non-riders probably must think that we are completely out of our minds. Why risk the danger? For riders such as me, it's a temptation that's impossible to resist.

The advantage I have is I don't have any kids. It's just me, and that's always been a factor.

My parents raised me to think independently. I've always been doing my thing, though most of the time extremely recklessly and irresponsibly. I might add that since I moved to Buena Vista, the Bell family has kind of adopted me and tried to do all they can for me. I try to do the same for them.

So, I'm out on the drive. I was a little tired. Cruising up the road, I was enjoying the nice day. Entering the canyon, there's the Comanche drive-in theater, which is a Buena Vista landmark. My tires were still just warming up. I was getting things rolling, taking in the scenery.

I didn't need any problems with police. I didn't need any problems with the sheriff. I didn't need problems from anybody. Yes, there is risk. Have I outrun the sheriffs before on this pass? Absolutely. But, the bottom line is I'm trying to convey true feelings about respecting law enforcement and the people, too. You just can't go ripping through these neighborhoods; that's what the open road is for.

The day was looking fine, no clouds in the sky, going to be gorgeous. I passed the sign, "San Isabel National Forest / Buena Vista Watershed."

Even a truck would do real good here in your take-a-right sweeper. You know I was going to accelerate. Looking over the weather conditions, it was a weekday morning and nobody was there, so it was a good time to charge the pass.

Coming into a right and left as I went up there with a blind right, I de-accelerated. I'd probably downshift two gears at this point. There was a lot of congestion. Cottonwood Hot Springs is located here, so you just need to be cool because people take a blind left coming out of there. Probably take it in third gear. Visor up.

Visor down, I prepared to accelerate. There was a real sharp right and then left, but there's a bridge there and it kind of pitches you straight. I went through some S-curves, downshifted. These are tricky corners. Right sweeper, accelerated up two gears. After a nice acceleration, I'd probably downshift two gears on the Beemer, taking a real nice left and a nice right in third gear. I came up in the traffic so I backed off. After a nice sweeper right, there were beautiful aspen tunnels, up, up, a little acceleration. There was a car I hoped would take a left at Cottonwood Lake.

I came into a sweeper left and also into a nice right, probably in fourth gear or a low fifth, and downshifted into a straightaway. Cottonwood Pass starts to open up a little bit, and continues to do so as elevation climbs. I wouldn't want to haul the mail around these driveways because of the traffic and incline. We have some rolling elevation here.

The next corner was a great, responsible spot to open up the bike. I let off the accelerator, dropped a gear, put my knee down, accelerated to the apex of the turn coming into a sweeper left – but remained calm and cautious because of the road up on the left.

God, the aspen trees were just phenomenally beautiful. Climbing up the pass, there was lots of visibility. Rainbow Lake was on the left. A slower car let me by; that was really nice of them. There was a sweeper right then sweeper left, then apex, then lining up, shifted up gear, maintained acceleration, and the brakes were nice and heated up at this point. I had to cool down because of parking lots, the avalanche parking area, then up to Denny Creek. A nice left swept into a right, setting up for an open straightaway. Fifth, fourth, dropping gears, pulling up high, 6,000 or 7,000 RPMs screaming through there, shift up, shift up, coming into this wide-open straight and then into a section with a right, a left, a blind right and a straightaway.

From there I got into the tight S-curves. There was an asphalt deviation right there I had to be careful of. I didn't want to unbalance the motorcycle at that point and had to be cautious. There's a right and then a beautiful wide-open left sweeper turn that I could easily push to 90 mph but am just ripping 80 to 85, a great place to accelerate. I came into a right, downshifted, heavy front brake, light rear brake. It sweeps out and there's a combination left that's like the Watkins Glen racetrack, and then into a corner that is bad ass. I came out of this corner and up this hill with smooth acceleration up through the gears up the hill. The campgrounds would probably be closed, but I needed to be cautious about them as I opened up the bike full throttle.

This section is one of my favorites. After a right sweeper that slopes left, I hit the apex and enter more turns as I accelerated up the mountain, climbing up a real nice grade. There's a wide-open setup for a left downshift, possibly even two gears because Denny Creek may be congested. Dive bombing past there is uncool because there's people in the parking lot about to go hiking or relaxing or whatever.

The ride starts heating up here. This pass has a wide-open, half-mile incline with a long sweeper left where you can get full acceleration.

I catch up with a pickup truck so I have to cool it. This is where the real turns start, and care is needed. I take a nice right and then a sweeper left through a stunning vista of the valley, with trees lining the mountains.

There's another parking area and this is where a prime series of curves are. They're like the specially designed curves called chicanes at the Formula One track at Imola, Italy. They can be dangerous. It's an awesome place for an auto racing or motorcycle enthusiast.

I ripped up the hill. There's a lot of visibility with the trees being narrow on the side of the road. A sloping right downshift leads to the turn. I went from third into second. The bike labored through this area. I dropped it into first, upshifted to second, and tried to get the bike into third. Most times around this corner, I would already be in third, then second, and try to get the bike back into third with full acceleration as I prepared for the next corner.

What I looked for in this corner was a braking point. Usually, on these turns, there are signs with arrows and road marks that are basically braking points. Rolling by Ptarmigan Lake trailhead parking area, a good place to take a hike, I swept left and right again. There was some messed-up asphalt right there and I had to be careful going into another series of curves. I entered an aggressive last hook into a deep right turn in first gear, then second gear, smooth acceleration going around the turn.

Specifically, I was going northbound on CR 306, about 14 miles west of U.S. 24, according to the local newspaper.

Ahead was a big left followed by a right. Going through the left, I blew it with the shift lag and my brakes locked up. My wheels squealed. The mistake sent me over the side of the road, 80 feet down the slope of a ravine.

Game over.

Formula One racing team operator Sir Frank Williams, one of the most successful in the business, said, "As a little boy, for a start, I enjoyed speed, too. That is why I finished up in a chair, for going too fast." In the 1980s, he was en route to the airport in a rental car when he failed to make a sharp curve, wrecked, and was paralyzed from the neck down and confined to a wheelchair.

The law of averages caught up with Sir Frank, and it caught up with me, too.

From (right) Buena Vista, Colorado, to the top of Cottonwood Pass (left). (Made by Tom Bell using Google Earth)

The curve where Mike crashed and was rescued along Cottonwood Pass. (Made by Tom Bell using Google Earth)

The skid mark on Cottonwood Pass, off CR 306, showed Mike's path off the road. (courtesy Tom Bell)

Top: A promo photo of Mike's 2006 BMW.

Above: Mike's bike after the crash.

Left: The bike's punctured gas tank.

Above: Curves on Cottonwood Pass, Mike's favorite ride in the country.

Below: Mike landed in this ravine with a tree on top of him and his 800-pound motorcycle on top of that.

Closer
views of the
ravine
where Mike
was
rescued on
June 9,
2015.

Above: Mike (right) meets Dave Bott, the cyclist who spotted Mike's skid mark leading off the road and initiated the rescue. Below: Paramedic Diana Wacker worked on Mike at the crash scene.

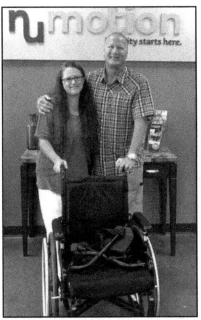

Left: Margo at NuMotion helped Mike find a wheelchair to use when not wearing his prosthetic left leg.

Above: This painting of children skating on a frozen pond hung in Mike's room at the rehab center. It reminded him of life outside his walls.

Above: Margaret Stone (left) and Carol Josich (right) worked with Mike in rehab, helping him stand and learn to walk again.

Above: Mike with flight nurse Meg Vito.

Below: Mike with pilot Travis Durbin.

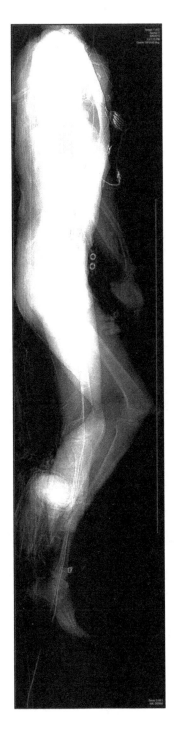

Left: CT scan shows missing left leg. Below: My left shoulder and left fibula and tibula.

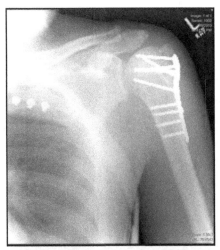

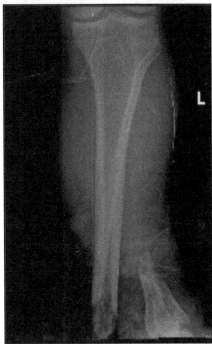

Mike Gallagher with Reggie and a copy of his book. Reggie forced Mike to get out of bed after returning home from rehab.

PART TWO:

The Rescue

Chapter Three
The Rescue

I really can't remember when I was rescued. The reports said it was about noon on June 9, 2015.

I remember just laying down there, and I was trapped. After I assessed my situation and came to that conclusion, I reached up and put my hand on the Sacred Heart badge on my gas tank and I said one prayer: the 23rd Psalm. Each phrase of it took a different meaning than I'd previously held.

> The Lord is my shepherd; I shall not want.
> He maketh me to lie down in green pastures: He leadeth me beside the still waters.
> He restoreth my soul: He leadeth me in the paths of righteousness for His name's sake.
> Yea, though I walk through the valley of the shadow of death, I will fear no evil: for Thou art with me; Thy rod and Thy staff they comfort me.
> Thou preparest a table before me in the presence of mine enemies: Thou anointest my head with oil;

my cup runneth over.
Surely goodness and mercy shall follow me all the days
of my life: and I will dwell in the house of the Lord
forever.

Thank God, I was not in extreme pain. Because of all the circumstances, I had not bled out and, for some reason, did not go into shock. Maybe I had, but I'm not a medical expert. As you will see, the injuries were extreme.

It was very important for me to have faith in a Higher Power. As best as I can recall, I had a calm, serene attitude. Maybe I relaxed knowing that the Lord was going to put me on the path of his choosing.

It's probably a good thing that I don't remember any parts of the rescue, even though I was apparently conscious and talking to emergency personnel.

A miraculous aspect of this story is that everybody connected with this rescue had their game on at the highest level. If they hadn't, this story would've had a very different outcome. Once again, I cannot thank the emergency services of Chafee County enough. From tip to tail, its work was above outstanding. Its members' expertise is the only reason I'm writing this today.

It should be noted that search-and-rescue can be as tough on the rescuers as war is for soldiers. Bad assignments can result in serious post-traumatic stress.

By the time work on this book is nearing completion three years after my accident, I've found that most of the search-and-rescue team members who saved me have left the business.

In approaching these folks to talk about my rescue, I found that some were excited and eager to share their memories, finding the experience cathartic. Others told me they were uncomfortable or just avoided me. I respect their decisions, and still appreciate them.

***

Dave Bott was the man who found me.

Before I met Dave during my rehabilitation, all I heard were fantastic things about him: local science teacher, proud parent and heavily involved in community activities. He also had first-responder training.

I was extremely nervous to meet Dave because he was solely responsible for saving my life.

Dave is a bicyclist. He rides regularly. Sometime after I crashed – initially, we thought as long as two days later but it may have been just a few hours – Dave was on his exercise route, driving his bicycle along the road that I had left.

He saw my skid mark and looked over the edge of the ridge. He went into action immediately, using his emergency training.

In interviewing Dave, I found him to be a wonderful and intense individual. I know that it took all of that intensity for him to not only find me but to be able to quickly diagnose my medical situation with the second person on scene, a mystery doctor from, we thought, Gunnison, Colorado. It's understatement to say that their quick wits and execution saved my life.

I heard a lot about Dave Bott, initially, from my friend

Dave Vogler at Buena Vista Drug. As information gets around this town, we tend to realize we're within a couple degrees of separation from most people in the area.

The dedication and safe spirit of the community of Buena Vista, Colorado, I think, is strong due to the fact that many of the folks in emergency services seem to have either grown up or went to high school here or maybe trained somewhere else but became deeply grounded into the community.

I hope you find the following interview with Dave Bott interesting. It was the first time I ever met Dave and heard his side of the story. We met at a local coffee shop in downtown Buena Vista.

Chapter Four
Bicyclist Dave Bott

D AVE BOTT: When you ride the pass, you see skid marks. When I rolled over your skid mark, there was no way to see down where you were, as you think and probably recollect. Because I am sure you had to look up and try to get someone's attention at some point. I don't know if you could see the road but it's banked enough that even me on the white line on the right side of the road on that switch back, you can't see down in that ditch in that little space.

MIKE GALLAGHER: (Referring to a hand-written map) Where are we at?

DAVE: Here is Ptarmigan Lake parking area, so you're heading up the pass, and you hit the first one and do this number and then it goes like that and you were right here. Your skid mark was 30 feet straight, so not your typical trailer or whatever. You can see, too, for whatever reason on any given day, there might be some little weird skid mark.

Somebody took off fast in this direction and I don't often make much of it, but when I came around I was pretty certain I hadn't seen that in any of my previous rides that week. I didn't make much of it when I saw it, so I went up past the switchback. I am headed up! I am in my zone!

But it just looked funny to me and then these thoughts started forcing me in my head to check it out. For some reason, that was really bothering me. I kept riding. I even went around the next switchback up the road, and I just kept thinking about it, which is rare. It's not rare for me to notice something, but it is rare for me to fester on something. I know that I don't ever turn around for any reason.

Just like I was saying, I'm hunting down a split. I have to get up there before the rain and get back down, but I could not shake it. I was about to go up the next switchback, and it was like, "I am just going down for a look," so I turned around and went back down.

It was so steep you could not see down there, riding by. I came right here (referencing the hand-written map), and laid my bike down in the gravel and started walking over. Within a second of peering down over the edge, I saw your helmet, the carnage and the bike, and I said, "Shit!"

I yelled down there, and you immediately responded, and I saw your head moving and I was like, "OK, here we go!" I scrambled down there in my road-biking shoes with carbon soles and big cleats.

***

DAVE: Before I go on, can you tell me what you think happened and when? Because I am very curious and always have been.

MIKE: When I would come into the first right-hander, I would sometimes be in first gear. The motorcycle would be wound up and then the shift to second, but just before that shift was a micro-second of lag between shifts.

As I approached this serious left-hand turn, I was going too fast and I just locked up both brakes. As you noticed, there was only a small skid mark. The best I can remember was the bike bucked me off, and the best I can guess was that I hit a tree and I looked up and the bike was coming down on top of me like a German engineered lawn dart. I put my arm up to flinch. Doing this resulted in my arm getting ripped off and wrapped behind my back.

I do not know if the engine was on top of my left leg, which I guessed was completely smashed. What I did was, when I was down there, it was like any other of the big crashes in my life, was I started trying to move fingers and limbs. I quickly realized I was trapped.

First of all, I had a lot of faith that everything was going to be OK. I know that sounds crazy. The bike was on top of me, and I could not move. I had use of my right arm, so I reached and picked up a rock and I said, "OK, I need to fight." With all of my energy, I threw that rock maybe eight to ten feet and that was it. I wasn't going to be able to get rocks on the road.

Then, as I was lying there, I noticed the gas started to leak out of the bike. I remember lying there, and what I would do was when I heard a vehicle coming up or down the pass, I would flip open my visor and yell as loud as I could. Then the car would go by. I would flip the visor down, realizing that the cars were accelerating and probably had their windows up.

But, I was going to keep on fighting no matter what. Most importantly, I refused to defecate in my pants and that was a big deal too.

So, that is what I could put together.

DAVE: That all sounds right, given the way I found you.

And, you did hit the tree. I think you were still flying and you hit the tree. If you were bucked, you must have been still pretty close or attached to the bike in some way like hanging on because there was a pretty big gouge in the tree. That, I believe, was the first time the bike and or you made contact with anything down there because it is really steep. So, I think that somehow you were attached to the bike in some way.

You would not have had any time to think about anything but, "I had an accident." You could've hit the forest floor and then it hit the tree and came down. Because when I saw the gouge in the tree and you were under the bike. I was like, "Oh, man! His trajectory was all the way off the road," and boom you hit down here some way.

The first point of clarification is interesting. The bike wasn't touching you at all. Not at all!

You were here (referencing the hand-written map). There was a stand of trees all in here. There was a little creek running by and the big rocky screed slope was here.

Your head was here. Your body was going like this. Your left arm was totally twisted around your back, so right away when I saw you, I could tell that it was completely dislocated or fractured or both. You had some nasty discoloring in your hand because your fingers were poking out over here.

As soon as I got down there, and you're lying like this and the bike is like this. The gas tank was leaking on you.

There was this tree and the tree was five or six inches in diameter. It was super tight against you and the bike was on top of it!

You had somehow fallen down, maybe, before the tree and then the bike came down on top of the tree and the tree got caught in between you and the bike, as you recalled. Because of the small spacing, you thought the bike was on top of you but there wasn't a piece of bike touching you!

Do you remember trying to cut that tree? You were trying to saw the tree, big as it was, with your key! I mean, I get it. You were desperate. At some point or at some time, you were conscious to the fact that the tree was the problem.

When I got down to you, and you had nick marks and you had been at it for I-don't-know-how-long, but you made some progress. Not enough to get the tree cut. At some point you abandoned that task.

Your tennis shoe, I saw a tennis shoe on the forest floor, rubber side facing me and the opposite of you. When I first saw that, I said, "I hope to hell that tennis shoe fell off."

I started talking with you, and your body was facing this way and your legs were down here in some configuration back underneath the tree.

I started talking with you right away, and you were

conscious. I started to think at what level of shock you would be in.

As soon as I got a response, I started crawling around you taking vitals. Pretty low blood pressure. You had a pretty good pulse, but it was weak. You were talking pretty good though.

After getting that all assessed, I crawled back around the tree to see the rest of you, and that's when I saw your totally compound fracture of the tib-fib. It wasn't even attached! Somehow it was still attached to the shoe. As I got closer to look, there wasn't much or anything hanging on to the rest of the leg.

You said, "I have been down here for three days!" and I questioned that right away, but I could tell you were probably delirious.

As I got around you, I could see a lot of blood on the forest floor and it was old and your wound looked pretty old.

I was like, "I don't know how long he has been down here, but he has been down here a while," because you clotted off and there was a lot of dry, cold tissue down there and it was not fresh.

I came back around and started talking with you a little more. I told you that I was going to leave you because I am going to walk up to the road. I said, "Don't lose me. Don't spiral and I will be right back." I scramble back up and within 45 seconds, we got lucky with an elderly couple driving by and I flagged them down. "Go down the pass and get a phone signal to call 911 for everything Buena Vista Fire has because there's a super-bad motorcyclist accident on the pass. You got it?" "Yep, we got it" and off they went down the pass.

**

MIKE: The first emergency vehicles started showing 45 minutes later, which, when you factor the couple driving down from 10,500ft, making the 911 call, then for emergency departments having to scramble and drive as fast as possible on one of the more technically demanding roads in North America – 45 minutes, in reality, is extremely fast.

DAVE: I quickly went back down and I started to talk with you about whatever, just trying to keep you alert and communicating with me. I started to crawl around a little more just to see more injuries if I could, and noticed this massive hematoma on your chest. Super-bad bruising and inflammation there, in addition to the arm, in addition to the leg. Who knows what kind of internal injuries you might have at that time? Completely no idea about spinal injuries or head injuries.

Understandably, you wanted that bike off you, and you were barking at me about that.

"Sorry man, we're not moving anything on you, but the bike is not on top of you, the tree is," I told you. But, the gas was dripping and you were pretty concerned about that.

You were in shock and you were in pain and you were in the mind that you wanted that bike off you. I've had some medical training and I knew that even the slightest of movements would cause cold dead blood and tissues to be dislodged from any one of your internal and exterior wounds, and if that would be coursing through your blood

47

stream, you could have a massive heart attack from a clot or a clot in the brain. Either way, that was going to be it.

I got you to chill out on the whole bike thing, and you started to. I asked you if you lived in town or had family here. That is when you mentioned Tom Bell. I've known Tom and Nancy Bell since my Leadville days.

It was now a waiting game.

***

DAVE: I glanced up and there was another cyclist standing up on the road. He obviously saw my bike lying down and there was nobody near it or on it, so he stopped and went looking around. He saw me and asked what was going on.

I asked him if he had some water and he said he did. For some reason, I felt I couldn't go up and leave you. He brought down some regular water, which was good. We super carefully held your helmet for fear of neck and spinal injuries. We got you some water, and that was good. For whatever reason, he went back up. Then I also went back up ... because I saw this pickup truck that had been coming down the pass, stopped with his window down asking the second cyclist what happened. I went across the road to the pickup truck and he pulled over then came jogging up to me.

MIKE: That must be the mystery doctor from Gunnison.

DAVE: He asked me, "What's going on?" while he was looking down at what was going on. He immediately went back to his pickup truck and pulled a sleeping bag out of the back and then got a real focused look in his eyes and started asking me questions about what information I had on you.

What was going on? We got down there, and now it was just the two of us. He starts checking you out really closely and telling you to do this and not to do that. You started telling him, "Get this bike off me," and he was like, "Nope."

It was a full five minutes before he revealed his profession. He told you not to worry. He was a medical trauma doctor, military trauma doctor with many tours in Iraq or Afghanistan or both. He is a trauma doctor who, I believe, works out of the Gunnison Emergency Room.

I breathed a great sigh of relief when he made that announcement. I was like, "Sweet!" because your demeanor started to change by the time I got to you. Initially, you were still pretty much fresh, fired up. You started to relax a little bit too much. That trauma doc told you, "You need to stay with us. You're thinking it is going to be OK, but it is not. You're starting to relax too much."

He was trying to get you focused, and I was picking up on that and it made sense to me. This is the cool thing about that trauma doc, and this is what we know about him.

Your situation was complicated enough from a medical standpoint and from an extraction standpoint, because of the bike and the tree. There was no way you were going to get moved until the tree was gone. The tree could not be moved until the motorcycle was blocked and tackled or removed. There was going to be a seriously bad domino effect if whatever we were going to do didn't go correctly. If everything came tumbling down on you, there would be no way to get you out without ending up with a more life-threatening condition.

***

DAVE: There were two teams that arrived. A paramedic team came down and they started assessing you. The trauma doc from Gunnison, without identifying himself right away, started rifling off everything that he assessed. They quickly figured out he was way medically trained.

Your situation was complex enough medically that I remember there being discussions about, "What should we do?" Not that they didn't know, but there were several options as to keep your body functioning properly while this obvious extraction took place.

There were two paramedics down there kind of the whole time. The Gunnison doc was quickly driving the conversation, and not shy about doing so, and they were in agreement with everything he was saying. I remember that clearly.

I was holding the hot and cold saline bag so you were already receiving fluid intravenously, and they had become a team of three working on you.

The other team, Chaffee County Fire, got down there. They noticed and told us about the gasoline around because they were talking about getting that tree out of there.

They made a wise decision. They couldn't use chain saws because of spark so they came with this massive cutting tool that's either pneumatic or hydraulic. It's not the Jaws of Life; it's a massive cutting tool with one-inch lines on both ends of the handle coming all the way down the side to cut the tree. They knew that they had to get that tree removed, but first we had to block and tackle the bike and get it suspended.

When they did cut the tree, it was like, "Whish!" It was a

sizable tree, 4- to 6-inch diameter pulled back and away. It was another fifteen or twenty minutes because that was extremely tricky.

Then the two teams were talking about what was going to be step one. As soon as the bike is up, step two: Cut the tree. Step Three: Dave, you have to move with us. On three, we have to get the back-board underneath him without disrupting a lot of the injuries internal and compound.

It was kind of "ready, let's go!" so there were plenty of folks around at that point. One, two, three, pull! I had to scamper up those boulders and the helicopter was waiting at that point. Total time was about an hour.

We got you up on the pavement, and then we all went over to the chopper. I handed the bags off to the helicopter flight team and we walked away from the helicopter because it was crowded. (Showing a picture from the front page of the local newspaper, the Mountain Mail, Dave points out the mystery doctor from Gunnison) The guy right there is the Gunny doc, right there with you communicating with the helicopter flight team. He was super concerned for you during that moment in time. I don't remember for sure, but he said you had about a 50-50 chance of making it to Denver.

It was the disrupting of your systems that was the dicey part about this one. It was pretty quick at that point; you were up and out of there.

I will tell you, too, as I implied earlier, there were about five or six people who made decisions in a complex set of variables. If there were any different decisions made by any one of those people, whether it was the paramedics or Fire or me, the helicopter – if different decisions had been made, things could've gone real differently.

It was not a black-and-white situation for anybody, that was for sure.

***

DAVE: Another interesting thing for me was that you weren't in an easy place to put the chopper down, and I've had some experience with helicopter piloting.

I was on a ground team building huts for the 10th Mountain Division up in the mountains near Leadville, Colorado, and sometimes that is done with a helicopter. We went through one pilot because they were not skilled enough to do this running up and down gulches and dropping off bags at high elevation, in low-air density. Not every helicopter can do it. Not every pilot can do it.

There was this guy out of Fort Collins, Colorado, who was amazing on the sticks. He got all of that done and we were all super impressed with him. It was the first time when I realized that not all pilots are cut from the same cloth, have the same skill set and all of that.

Your guy (Travis Durbin with EagleMed) got in and out of there, and did such a great job. That can't be easy putting a helicopter down in a place like that. Of course, there are no power lines to deal with, but there are always winds that are doing weird things and there are cars, trees. With one misstep, you could have had a second disaster on our hands. He got you up and out of there. It was really cool.

***

DAVE: I remember very well when I first got down there,

like I said, I didn't know how long you were down there and if your claim of three days was true but I gained at least a sense.

I asked you if it happened in the night just because of the way it happened. I am a good cyclist and I go faster than I should and I do it all the time, but I thought it happened at night in a lower visibility scenario.

You were very confident, though, that it happened during daylight hours. I knew that it was not that day. I was up there about eleven or before and I knew it wasn't that day because your wounds were not fresh. Both your internal bleeding and your tib-fib were not fresh. Your chest was like the size of two chests. You had a huge collection of fluids in your left side internal. You were at least there from the evening before, and I don't know when you left town. If you can pin that down it would help us.

MIKE: I think what I did was, I had a lot on my mind. My wonderful dog, Gertrude, got into some rat poison and I had to put her down and I was just beside myself. I think I went at dusk just a quick ride. It's beautiful. What a road. As I was coming up, I crashed, but I was stuck.

DAVE: It was probably evening? Maybe 14 hours, 16 hours-plus you were there. Your quote and my understanding was you had been there for three days was just your way of telling me, "Help me out! I might be cold, in shock and in incredible pain." Try to tell me your chronology.

I think it was a full 16 hours if not more, which is a long time to be in the condition you were in. To be able to watch cars go by and hear cars go by and know that time is slipping away, probably saying, "How long is this going to go on for?"

I am sure that went into your mind.

MIKE: It was obvious that I wasn't going anywhere, but I would flip that visor up and yell because that was how I was going to fight. I wasn't going to give up and I had faith that I was going to be rescued.

I had to keep hanging in there and do everything I could possibly try to save myself, which, at that point, was yell. The car would go by and I would flip the visor down and nod off or fall back to sleep or something. Hear another car, do the same thing over and over again.

***

DAVE: On a personal note, just out of curiosity, and you don't have to answer, but when you keep saying, "I had faith," was that your faith in your ability to do that? Was that the faith that someone would show up? Faith in God?

MIKE: Faith in God. I had a religious icon that I glued to my gas tank and it said, "This place will be blessed ..." I have a lot of faith in my Higher Power. He didn't make me suffer when I was down there. You saw how I was and I was comfortable, if that can be imagined. I think it all just overwhelmed me.

DAVE: The reason I ask is because of a completely secular point. I saw a skid mark and it bothered me and I turned around. I'm a person of faith myself. One of my friends called me a closet Christian. We are believers in the strongest, most significant sense that God is the number one peace within our lives. Christ is the number one reason we are together. It is all of our lives, and friends who are not believers, if I said something like this and they might hear that and say, "Hey do you have a nickel?" God is everything to me. I am a Christian of deep faith.

The little voice in my head was extremely atypical on a ride like that. I notice lots of things and have lots of thoughts. I look at weather and assess a lot of things. Like you, I am usually up there trying to own the road. Just have some mental flushing going on, and I do that by putting my body through pain on a bicycle. Get all those endorphins and all of those neuro-transmitters stable and happy. Serotonin and dopamine, that's where I get it, on a bicycle. I am usually way into my zone and I am really not paying attention to anything or anyone else. I have been doing it so long, I can tell what kind of truck or car is coming up by listening to be safe and that is about it. Otherwise, I am in a state that is nice to me. Not complicating things and I never turn around. I can be massively hailed on and I will press on every single time. It is my window, and that is what I want to do.

To this day, I never had a more powerful voice in a situation like that telling me to turn my bike around. "Go look. Turn around and go look. Turn around and go look." No, that's nothing. Just another skid mark like any other. I am on a good pace today. "Turn around and go look." It was really weird.

After enough of that, and I am sensitive to those voices, it was like, "OK, OK, I will turn around and go look. The heck with it." Someone not of faith might not understand what we are talking about, but I can assure you that it was not me that turned around. It was the Holy Spirt using me as a conduit to answer your prayer and to honor your faith position that everything was going to be OK. I think it could have been anyone who is sensitive to those voices, but it was your God.

MIKE: I have a whole bunch of guardian angels, and we don't have enough time to go into all of my accidents, but I have guardian angels there. I was staying calm despite very serious injuries and I wasn't suffering. I was not suffering! I knew that was funny about the key and the tree.

DAVE: That, actually, was not irrational, because, like I said, at some point you were very aware that the tree was a problem. I am sure we could go up there and I can show you the scar in the tree where you were trying to saw the tree with your key. You had gotten a quarter inch with a not-very-good-tool – a key, not even a good key. You did some damage with what you could. You had a sense that the bike was on you, and that the gasoline was troublesome to you.

MIKE: (Showing Dave the huge burn on my back.) That is a gasoline burn, full thickness. The gasoline was eating away at my flesh.

DAVE: It was cold down there, and that was another piece of your constitution and your tenacity. You were there all night and there was a creek running right next to you, within two feet. It was running in June and it was more than enough that if you came in contact with it, you'd have entered a hypothermic stage. You would've ended up a lot different than the way I found you. It wasn't deep enough to drown, but you'd have been too wet immediately and then your state of hypothermia would've been much more severe. With the injuries and hypothermia, it would not be good.

**

MIKE: I had a compound fracture of the left shoulder.

DAVE: So you had a compound on that arm? Well, I'm

not surprised because, if you can remember, I could not see that and they didn't even cut that away for me to see or any one of us to see that compound down there. When I first saw your fingers sticking out here and the color was like, "Man, that is broken!" A profound dislocation, but I felt pretty strongly that must be a fracture to get that contorted. It was really bad.

MIKE: The injuries where I had a compound fracture of my left shoulder (showing Dave the huge scar on my left shoulder), they told me the bones were sticking out.

DAVE: Not to be confused by your left leg?

MIKE: Right. Not to be confused by my left leg. Correct.

DAVE: I wonder if it was the top of the humerus sticking out, based on the scar. You said you broke a couple of vertebrae.

MIKE: I believe there were five broken vertebrae. That burn penetrated into my right lung, so I don't know how they fixed that up. (Skin grafts.) My left leg was obviously amputated below the knee. I am extremely grateful for that because above-the-knee amputations are more complicated by having a joint to deal with. I had 100 percent nerve damage on my right leg from the knee down. They call it "drop foot." It really doesn't move much at all. So, I guess the tree was on top of that too?

DAVE: The tree was in contact with you, increasingly from your torso down through your legs.

MIKE: They put me in coma. I was in coma for several weeks and they performed all the operations and procedures. Several dialysis treatments.

I guess that was about all I can remember.

DAVE: It would be really great if we can track down the "Mystery Doctor from Gunnison." I wanted to contact them and tell them what a stellar employee and individual they have on staff. Because of the way he conducted himself and his history, that went into your situation. I am sure he would say, "Hey, it's my job. This is what I do. This is what I have chosen to do, and this is what I did in the military."

But not everybody is up to the task. Every nurse, every teacher, every president of the United States, every doctor – they are not all the same. Each has various degrees of history and experience, compassion. All people bring a very specific skill set and passion. The mystery doc was on it, in a real intelligent way. Everyone on a compassionate level would want the best for you, but he was really sharp about the way he went about saving your life.

I can only tell you that he was a very active, all the Crested Butte and Gunnison people are super active. I can't remember if he had kayaks on his truck. I think he had two young children and his wife in the truck. They were on the way to vacation somewhere, I don't know where. Paddle the Ark (Arkansas River)? Young guy in his early forties to early fifties. It was either Afghanistan or Iraq. I know he did tours because he mentioned that to you to give you some confidence to convince you that you were in good hands.

You would listen to him and not worry about the bike and all that stuff. I know that about him. Good looking guy with curly dark hair. Maybe 170 pounds and a nice guy. Super nice guy.

***

DAVE: The most interesting thing was all of the different decisions I sensed could be made on how to execute, what to execute and when with that small team of emergency individuals. In my mind, that is a huge part of why you are here. It was like when I found you, it was like, "Holy Cow! This is not going to go well, even with help," because I knew enough after I assessed and saw what I did see. I didn't know about the vertebrae. I didn't know about the compound to your left shoulder. If I would've seen that, I would've said, "There was no way he is going to live. There is no way he is getting to an emergency room."

MIKE: What I think happened was the gas didn't just blow out, but it was just dripping on me.

DAVE: Oh, yeah, it was dripping on you when I got down there because you said, "Hey, there's gas dripping down here!" I was like, "Yeah, I see it."

MIKE: What may have happened was the gasoline cauterized the open wounds.

DAVE: You cauterized yourself on the leg because there was no gasoline down there. Everything on your left leg was torn apart. Any musculature and ligaments of any kind hanging on down there wasn't much. I got down there and said, "Crap!" I was hoping that shoe was off because it was parallel to your other leg. That was lucky that it cauterized on its own.

MIKE: People tell me how lucky I was and I know deep inside of me that it was my God, my guardian angels, taking care of me.

I know you can profess your faith through religious

organizations or as I do, by cherishing those moments with myself or with close or dear friends, which are few.

DAVE: We are the insensitive dolts who don't listen to Him and don't spend enough of our lives trying to hear that still-small voice and discern from our own conscience and all of these things. He is always there, always trying to communicate with us and ready to do so, but I believe that we all lead our own lives to go to lesser capacities, depending on who it is. Not being as sensitive to it as much as we should, and becoming distracted with the earthly aspects of our humanness and our problems. There are aspects of our faith which are weak and we don't trust Him in certain situations. We're at fault not to hear that voice more often.

I can tell you that He was talking to you that day and he was talking through me to you, using me and shouting at me as I proceeded up the pass.

OK, that's what I remember. I was like, "I am not turning around, I never turn around! Turn around and go look!" I just remember that and I had to hear it like 15 to 20 times before I obeyed, so I'm a little ashamed of myself for that because I want to say that I began to hear that as soon as I rolled over that skid mark.

That kind of ride is not real enjoyable for me. I know I go up there looking for it and that is why I have enjoyed the successes I have had, because I get a lot of enjoyment putting myself through a fair amount of agony to make a good ascent out of a ride on a given day. The fun thing for me is when I get up there and go, "Sweet! I am only two minutes off a good climb." That will work for me today.

Chapter Five
Doctors on Scene

As the rescue unfolded, it was actually key that Dr. Ruiter and Dr. Johnson arrived on scene. Just by chance, they were doing search-and-rescue training on top of Cottonwood Pass when they received the alert related to my accident. Arriving at the accident site, both Dr. Ruiter and Dr. Johnson assumed different roles in this accident. Dr. Ruiter established radio communications and Dr. Johnson went down into the ravine to help both Dave Bott and the mystery doctor from Gunnison. It is truly an understatement to say that these doctors used their training and professionalism to help coordinate this major rescue.

RUITER: My name is Rick Ruiter. I'm an ER physician in Salida (Heart of the Rockies Regional Medical Center), and I've been in Salida, Colorado, since 1999. I'm also a volunteer fire fighter and I also work with the Chafee County Fire Department.

On the day of the accident, my friend Doug (also a physician) and I were up at Cottonwood Pass hiking around and practicing snow-hiking techniques. On our way down, we received a page (at about 11:30 a.m.) from Salida dispatch regarding a motorcycle accident.

We were approximately five minutes away from the scene. We met up with the bicyclist and other bystanders. At that point, we found Mike off the bank and down into some trees, pinned down there by his motorcycle and some trees.

My role at the time was mostly communications, and at that time I did have my communications radio with me, so I worked with dispatch on communications regarding the arrival of the ambulance, the fire department personnel and helicopter.

I continued my role on communications throughout the entire time of the rescue. Actually, I did not go down the bank to take care of you, Mike. Doug did and I guess there was another doctor on scene who was taking care of you until the ambulance came.

The ambulance got there first, then the fire department got there shortly after, and the helicopter arrived after that.

JOHNSON: My name is Doug Johnson and I'm a retired obstetrician gynecologist. I practiced in Iowa for about 20 years and moved here to Chafee County in 1995, where I practiced at both Salida and Leadville hospitals as well as in Buena Vista for another 18 years. I have been with search and rescue for about 10 years and just last fall, after your accident, I joined Chafee County Fire as well.

As Rick said, we were up there doing some snow training

on top of Cottonwood Pass, and as we were coming down, the pager went off.

There was a woman there who was saying her husband was down with Mike and was an ER doctor. I went down the hill to find Mike, and he was in the extremely contorted position with a motorcycle and tree branches that were bent over, small trees on top of him, dripping gasoline on top of his leg.

We had gasoline dripping on him and he was pinned under an 800-pound BMW motorcycle. We weren't sure if you had been there two or three days and if that was accurate, but you were definitely there overnight.

There was a tire track which the bicyclist had seen, and it still visible today but he did not notice that the day prior, so he looked over the edge and found Mike.

Shortly thereafter the EMS people came and got an IV going and put him on some oxygen. We had to cut the tree but we were afraid to cut the tree down because of the gasoline and the spark from a chainsaw. We were successful at doing that. We lifted the tree off and slowly lifted the motorcycle. Only then could we remove Mike from the wreckage. We put Mike on a litter, and Fire came and sent down some ropes so with the ropes and the litter we were able to pull him up and into the waiting helicopter, which then took off.

Chapter Six

Paramedic Diana Wacker

I am Diana Wacker, and I moved around Chafee County on and off since 2007. I was a raft guide for the summers and full time after my paramedic school, and was lucky enough to get hired on by Chafee County EMS as a paramedic.

MIKE: What kind of medical school did you attend?

DIANA: Colorado Mountain College in Edwards, Colorado. I did a lot of mountain training there and started working as a part-time paramedic and was there for two years. Now, I'm full-time with Summit County, Colorado, ambulance. I still live here in Buena Vista, Colorado, full time. I have been a paramedic for 3 ½ years.

I believe we were at the station when we got the call, and I was probably making lunch when the call came. We started heading up the pass, and we got word that you were a quarter-mile to a half-mile past Ptarmigan Lake trailhead, so I knew exactly where you were and where we were headed.

En route, dispatch came over with the report of a gentleman on a motorcycle and that he was trapped underneath the motorcycle and been potentially there two days. Plus, the motorcycle was still crushing him.

At that moment, we knew we needed a helicopter, and actually there was a second call that Salida was running. I believe it was between Mount Antero and Mount Princeton and they called for a helicopter as well as Flight for Life out of Summit County because, first of all, they're the only helicopter that can transfer blood and I wouldn't know if you needed that until we got you un-trapped. I wanted them to avoid crossing over, but my boss got on the radio and said EagleMed was getting that call. OK, helicopter's coming out, so that's all I really could care about.

We got up there on scene, and Dr. Ruiter was up there with the radio, handling the radio traffic for us. First, I looked over the hill and I didn't see anything. Then I saw the motorcycle and I saw somebody underneath it. I quickly jumped back into the ambulance and I would not be able to carry down a lot of medical equipment because it spread out in the ambulance. Also, I did not want to go up and down that hill because it was at least 80 feet down. I grabbed the sodium bicarb and the calcium chloride and all of our RS I stuff into my pockets. I had an I/O in one pocket and all the drugs in another, then I walked down to see you.

When Chafee County Fire got on scene, I yelled up to them to throw a rope down and tie it to the sign so we could walk up and down that hill without any more problems.

I did my typical response and you responded with your name, Mike. I knew, OK, he's responsive. Did a quick feel on your head and there weren't any head injuries and that wasn't a problem. The right arm was the only one moving, and I couldn't even see where your left arm was, so we started cutting off your clothes and getting a bunch of blankets to cover you up with.

I couldn't see which leg it was; all I can see is a tib-fib sticking out and up underneath the bike. At that point, I didn't know if it was the right foot or the left. I just knew it was a partial amputation and that the gas was, actually, the gas tank was leaking down into the wound. We saw that and we knew we were going to have to deal with it fast.

MIKE: (I showed Diana my back scar and explained to her it was a full-thickness burn, which apparently collapsed my lung as a result of pooled gasoline slowly burning the flesh.)

DIANA: At that point, we couldn't roll you, and I pretty much had the upper chest to work with. You were in excruciating pain.

I got my partner and got an IV in your AC. As soon as I got that, I pushed about 200 Fentanyl, and you started to calm down. It was nice to have you not screaming in pain, and I know that doesn't last that long. You looked at me and said, "Get this bike off me!" I put my hand on your chest, looked you straight in the eye and said, "I can't right now. I have to stabilize you before I move this bike because if I move this bike right now, it will probably kill you."

Once I said that, you said, "OK, take your time." Part of the stabilization that I needed to get was establishing an IV getting fluids going, put a heart-rate monitor on you and the pads on you so when we pulled the bike off, you didn't go into cardiac arrest.

We had all of that, and coordinating with where Fire was at and how many branches needed to be cut or moved before we'd be able to move you.

One member of the flight crew showed up, Aaron, the flight crew paramedic. I told him what I saw and what I thought and that we needed to give you some sodium bicarb and potentially calcium chloride, in which case we'd give you a second IV. We couldn't do that in the same line so pulled the IO out and put an IV in your humerus.

MIKE: What is the difference between an IO and an IV?

DIANA: The IV is just a needle catheter that goes in your vein and goes directly into your bloodstream. The IO goes into the bone, which has the same amount of blood flow circulation we were able to give you all the drugs through it because we might have to put a second line in your neck. But the I/O is quick, usually guaranteed. They usually go into the leg, but your legs were still entangled so that wasn't an option. Once we got a line going, we still mainly use the IV because it flows better, but if we need a secondary line, there is another option.

We coordinated with Chafee Fire and we had a tourniquet ready to put on whichever part of the leg was sticking out. When we got the motorcycle off you, the bike was sitting on top of your pelvis and it looked pretty obvious that it had been cutting off the circulation and that was controlling the bleeding. As soon as we got that off, you'd potentially start to bleed again, but the biggest concern that I had was because the motorcycle was sitting on top of your pelvis and your left arm being stuck underneath you for the amount of time we assumed you had been there and anything longer than eight hours and we knew that it was longer than that - we were very concerned about a crushing injury because the compression happens when the tissues below start to die in the cells and releases potassium, and the potassium will get back into your bloodstream and travel to your heart and kill you very quickly.

We were very concerned about hyperkalemia sensitivity and our treatments for that are sodium bicarb and calcium chloride. We were not ready to give you the calcium chloride because once we had you on a monitor and everything had to look just right before we moved the bike. We had decided with Aaron, the other paramedic, that we would give the sodium bicarb, lift the bike off you, and put the tourniquet on you.

When Chafee Fire gave us the OK, that's when we pushed the sodium bicarb to try and neutralize it. We then lifted the bike off you and Aaron put the tourniquet on you because he was in a good position for that. He realized that it was your left leg that was amputated. We got the tourniquet on and then pulled you onto the guys to do the lifting and moving, but I was still very concerned with your cardiac, with the hyperkalemia. I was pretty sure that I was carrying the heart-rate monitor and by the time we got up to the helicopter, I was praying for the helicopter. I could already see your T-waves on your EKG were starting to peak more than what you had initially, which was telling me that there was some hyperkalemia.

MIKE: Could you explain what hyperkalemia is?

DIANA: High potassium and low potassium is very important to the heart and you have to have the right levels. Too high or too low are very bad.

MIKE: Just to inform you, at the hospital, I was diagnosed with a lacerated kidney and I don't know if that was leaking potassium into my blood system.

DIANA: Yes, we could not tell, but we had a high suspicion that there were some internal things going on, but without an MRI, you could not tell. I think that every ounce of you hurt so we couldn't really push to tell.

MIKE: I do not remember any of that. I remember crashing and yelling at Dave Bott to get the motorcycle off of me or just move it a little bit and he said he could not move it.

DIANA: Because you were talking the whole time and about the lack of medication, I was trying to keep you as comfortable as possible, knowing that there were a lot of things potentially going on. Your left shoulder, and somebody told me your rib cage was crushed, and then I listened to your lung sounds and you had good lung sounds and your blood pressure was great, so I wasn't concerned about that.

At that point, looking at your left shoulder and moving it, it was so swollen. I didn't know if it was broken or it wasn't. When we got to the hospital, it was obvious that it was completely dislocated. But you were on it so long that I could not see much of the arm, but I could see a lot of the swelling on the left side of your chest.

It was very red and just initially looked real bad. I kind of poked around and plodded on it, but the lung sounds were OK so I was like, OK, I'm not going to worry about that now because there were other things to worry about.

As we pulled you up, you had good pulses in the right arm, but you had no pulses in your left arm or any pulses in your right leg. Whether or not there were any, I didn't feel any, so I was pretty convinced that you would end up with just one limb – that right arm, because of the amount of time you were crushed and without blood flow. They probably could not save them. It was definitely disconcerting.

MIKE: Initially, they wanted to amputate the left arm and amputate the right leg from the knee down. I have 100-percent nerve damage on my left arm from the shoulder and 100-percent nerve damage in my right leg from my knee down.

DIANA: But you still have it?

MIKE: Apparently, my friend Tom Bell drove down to St. Anthony's. I think they wanted the easy way out because of my condition and just amputate the limbs. Tom insisted that he wanted my limbs saved.

The next question I have is – from what I gather, it was a pretty intense scene – how would you rate the rescue on a scale of one to ten?

DIANA: At that point in my career, it seemed pretty much the norm for me because I was basically the shit magnet for a while. Every scene was like that to me.

Things seemed to have calmed down for me, and that's really nice. On an honest scale of one to ten? I hate to say it, but we sometimes are just an expensive taxi for a lot of people and, as morbid as it sounds, dead people are actually very easy. You can't make them more dead. Then, there would be people who are trying to die on us.

We are trying to do everything we actually can rapidly but not too fast, to avoid mistakes that would cause more damage but knowing that time is crucial and you have to get them out there. I guess you were a nine. Plus, the location of it was rugged, and once we all got down there, you couldn't move around very easily, and we all had our little spots. I was up near your head and Mark was down by your arm and the trauma doc (from Gunnison) was between us on your right side, and he was just awesome.

We got you up to the helicopter. I couldn't tell if your leg was amputated because your pants were kind of holding things together. I was saying to myself, "At least, let's get them in line," because it was just lopped off. I remember picking up a shoe that was just not connected, so I put it in its place where it should go, then we wrapped you up and placed you in the helicopter.

Chapter Seven

The Firemen: Brian Welch & Chris Stromer

B RIAN WELCH: I am Brian Welch. Career (fire inspector and firefighter) with Chafee County Fire and I have lived in this county since March 2002 and have been a firefighter since April 2002.

I am trying to remember much about the scene. We got the page for motorcycle over the edge on Cottonwood Pass and trapped. We've been to a lot of motorcycle accidents and I don't think we ever had come across a motorcyclist trapped. They usually get thrown well away from their bike, and it was just a matter of scooping them up and putting them in the ambulance and off they go.

CHRIS STROMER: I am Chris Stromer. I have grown up in Chafee County. I moved out of the county and came back in 2007. Started career firefighting here with Chafee County Fire, but first I was a volunteer and I started my career three years ago.

I was trying to remember the scene. We heard en route that it was a motorcycle injury and was trapped. He could've been up there possibly a couple days.

BRIAN: Yes, that is right. They mentioned you had been up there a day or a day and a half. Maybe two days. No one was sure.

MIKE: What I'm going to show you gentlemen is what we refer to as Map A. This shows the 30-foot skid mark.

CHRIS: Yup, right in to one of the signs, it actually looked like you clipped the signpost.

MIKE: Clipped that little sign, and then ended up somehow flying down there and hit a tree and then the tree came down on top of me.

BRIAN: There is a creek right down there by your feet.

MIKE: My left arm was ripped off, so this signifies my arm being ripped off, and there is my helmet. Any of that help refresh your memories?

BRIAN: I remember EMS got there first and so did one of our volunteer firefighters, Dr. Rick Ruiter. He is an ER doctor in Salida. I think he was in the area already, heard the page, and got there 10 minutes before us.

We didn't know the extent of your being trapped and the extent of your injuries. EMS got there before us and somebody had initiated medical flight. It was definitely Mark Willborn, EMT basic, and Diana was the helicopter paramedic.

CHRIS: I do remember you were trapped under the tree

and the motorcycle was on top of the tree and that was actually pinching your leg. I was pretty much responsible for getting the saw out and cutting the tree.

BRIAN: I remembered we and Mark started setting up for just a simple, safe, get-you-up in a Stokes basket. Have a line tethered to you so we don't drop you further down the hill, creating more problems for you. We hadn't really even tied in with EMS. Dr. Ruiter had us getting set up to bring you up in a Stokes basket. We parked near the scene, and I remember we are getting set up for a kind of low-angle rescue. EMS paramedic Mark Willborn yells up to me, "Hey, Brian, you have to come down. You need to see this."

I started seeing some of the issues. Mark says, "He's trapped." You were trapped, and I looked and started noticing, "OK, we got a bike on you," and then we have trees coming up through either wheel wells and the forks.

CHRIS: You are kind of twisted on your left side. The bike was pushing that tree, bending down and over you.

BRIAN: What we were finding was that the issue was like, "OK, simply cut the tree and move the bike." Well it didn't take long for us to figure out that if you cut the tree supporting this 800-pound bike, it was going to drop right on top of you. I don't think the bike was actually touching you at all. I think the bike was crushing a sapling over your pelvis.

EMS was doing their thing, and they were concerned about compartment syndrome as soon as we start moving stuff because you had pulse in one out of four limbs. I remember seeing the arm that was underneath you completely blue and purple and it was just lifeless, nothing to it, and your leg was cut in half.

CHRIS: Your leg was severed at the shin.

BRIAN: I don't remember the other one that well, but you had access and one good hand, your right one. EMS was real concerned about compartment syndrome.

MIKE: What is compartment syndrome?

BRIAN: My understanding of it is basic, and the EMT and paramedics could help you out a little bit better than I. You stop the blood supply to a limb and all of a sudden it becomes toxic, if you will. It doesn't get cleaned through the rest of your system.

I think it becomes acid, toxic with the buildup of carbon dioxide and as soon as you relieve that pressure and all that blood gets pumped back into your body and it's too much to handle at once. They had to, I believe, use sodium bicarb as soon as they started allowing the blood back into your system. They pump you full of sodium bicarb, which should neutralize the acidosis in your blood and not kill you instantly.

There were a couple times where, had we messed up or EMS messed up, you could've been much worse off than before. If we allowed that bike to drop on top of your pelvis, potentially a broken pelvis? I don't know if you had any pelvis issues with your injuries?

MIKE: There were, I believe, six broken vertebrae.

BRIAN: OK, yeah, we could not have that bike come down on top of you because it would have caused a lot more damage. They, the EMS, know a lot more about that, so I called Chris down. He's our "mechanical guy." We started working through the problem of how we cut the tree because the tree had to be cut. Two had to be cut.

CHRIS: We worried about the fuel spill and possibly igniting the fuel spill, so we thought of what we were going to use. Thinking about using cutters to cut the tree but we didn't want it to twist the tree. There were a couple trees that were not in the way.

BRIAN: We got a couple of the trees out of the way. They were kind of holding everything together, either directly in the way of getting the bike off you or holding the bike up, so we used both the cutters and a chainsaw.

CHRIS: We had to be very coordinated with the people holding the bike stable so it didn't fall down further, like we said. That was an amazing effort! Straps around the bike. People could not lean over the bike to grab the handle bars and get a better hold on it. We were very cautious not to let the bike lay on you any further. We had about three or four people, and I was holding the rear tire of the bike off the ground.

BRIAN: I was kind of in the creek, about to pull it off you, toward the creek.

CHRIS: Trying to coordinate that and getting you out at the same time.

BRIAN: Right, and we found out that we made it work. It was really easy. You know how your engines kind of come out a little bit? What we were able to do is get some 2x4s and 4x4s, box cribbing, and built up a platform to eventually meet that engine.

CW: We were able to cantilever it off that.

BRIAN: Cantilever off that, as opposed to lifting an 800-pound motorcycle. We stood in the creek and flopped it this way and built that box cribbing in the creek, kind of underneath your engine.

MIKE: Where was the creek? (We reference map A.)

CHRIS: The creek came down this way and I want to say you're what was right in here, and that's where we built the cribbing. Right here underneath you was the engine, and then we were able to get the tree, like I said, up like that across this side and then we put the straps right here. Strap around the handlebars to pull up to stabilize the wheel, and we were both standing in the creek. I think we had one person on the side while EMS coordinated with us to pull you out.

BRIAN: It was definitely one of the most difficult motorcycle calls we have ever been on. We have been on a few vehicle extractions that just literally took hours to get the last person out of the vehicles – not because we didn't know what we were doing, but because when little cars get hit by big semis, things get mangled all around people and it takes forever.

I was amazed how little blood there was anywhere around you, and I got the impression that the tree and the way the bike landed on it kind of cut off the circulation and was beneficial.

CHRIS: Hard to believe that there are all kinds of critters and animals up there, but you were never bothered by them. That was awesome. Just that mentality of thinking what that must've been like for you laying down there for all that time, it was hard to think about.

BRIAN: We realized how if you were another 6 inches closer to the creek, getting your feet wet overnight at that altitude would've sent you hypothermic real quick. I think that would've become a different outcome.

That was quite the ordeal, so we had a couple guys stay up top coordinating the helicopter coming in. I think it was Marty Johnson and he came up with the brush truck. He has been a career deputy sheriff and a volunteer for us. I believe he was the one coordinating the landing zone for the helicopter, and getting that in was key.

CHRIS: And Bob Meyer was there.

BRIAN: The captain was up there on the bank, but he didn't go down. It was quite interesting.

CHRIS: We did set up the ropes.

BRIAN: I think we were able to hand him up and slowly move him, but we had him on a belay line and a safety line. We did not want him to tumble down the slope again.

It was amazing that, afterward, looking at it, I remember seeing where you were and then right there was a big fir tree, a 6- to 8-inch fir tree. You could see it was where I was standing down at the creek and was probably head height or higher where you hit it and bounced back a little bit – there was a section of bark taken off, and I bet that is where you impacted. I bet you can find that today.

CHRIS: Yes, there was another tree around there too, I can't remember.

BRIAN: That's the one you hit that brought you straight down on top of the other trees.

CHRIS: It was such a blessing that everything lined up. That bicyclist to be able to recognize and check on something like that was and is, wow, like awesome.

How many cars had passed by and it would not be a place where you would want to stop – you know, a blind corner you can't see around. I snowmobile up here in the winter and I've nearly of gone off that on a snowmobile, but it gets me thinking about snowmobiling in the winter and how easy it would be to come down there off the side and not be seen. I think I've been snowmobiling up there for years and years. I graduated high school from here.

BRIAN: Are the skid marks still there?

MIKE: Only if you know what to look for.

Chapter Eight
Helicopter Pilot Travis Durbin

I am Travis Durbin and I was born in central Missouri. Raised there, grew up there. Started flying at 17 years old and knew that's what I wanted to do. From that, I went into the Marine Corps and ended up working on helicopters. I moved from there and transitioned from the Marine Corps to the Army to fly helicopters. I did that for about 10 years.

I left the Army and started flying EMS back in Missouri as an air medevac. Then went from there, did some time back in the military as a contractor but went back to EMS because I missed it: the schedule, the mission and all of that, came back to it. I went to Med Trans, which is another AMGH company (Air Medical Group Holdings). While I was there, we were working on putting this base in Salida, Colorado. From there, I went to EagleMed when they opened up the base. Earlier this year, in the beginning of March, we moved to Reach. I have now worked for all four of the AMGH companies.

Mike Gallagher: What is AMGH?

TRAVIS: Air Medical Group Holdings. It is the big umbrella company that owns all the air medical companies I have worked for. Med-Trans, EagleMed, Air Evac and Reach. So that's kind of how I got here.

MIKE: Thousands and thousands of hours training plus mission air time! Wow!

(Author's note: It's amazing to know that Travis was the helicopter pilot. We all agree that a lesser-skilled pilot would've never thought about landing up there on the road. It saved a lot of time by not shuttling me down the pass in an ambulance then transferring me to the helicopter in a field near Buena Vista. I would've never made it. Plus, I discovered there were two helicopter rescues that same morning with other pilots that were scrambled. I believe God picked Travis to be my pilot.)

TRAVIS: Moving on with that day, it started out with a phone call from the EMS director to my pilot phone directly to let us know that they were going to be calling us. That is something that we did in Salida just because we were so far from the helicopter, to shorten the time and get us to the helicopter as quickly as possible.

We headed out to the helicopter, but we didn't really know what we were getting at that point. Then we got a call from our dispatch putting us on standby. The information we got at that point was that it was a motorcycle accident and they believed you had been down there several days at that point, near Cottonwood Pass.

We received the coordinates. From that, we got the launch, and headed your way.

Originally, we were told that you were on a trail near Cottonwood Pass, so we were thinking this was some kind of a dirt-bike accident not a road-bike accident. We were looking at some off-road trails off of Cottonwood Pass then we finally established radio communication with the guys on the ground. We were able to find them and they just happened to be where you were at. In that corner it was a hard spot to see them from where we were; even though we were only a mile away, we couldn't see them down in those trees. Once we knew where they were, they guided us in and we came in and landed right down there on the road.

At that point, the crew, I believe it was Aaron, went out to meet with EMS. I believe Dr. Ruiter was there, standing up above where you were at, down below.

MIKE: Technically, Dr. Ruiter was handling all communications. There was a sheriff's deputy who coordinated the landing zone. It was brought to my attention how important the LZ (landing zone) was.

TRAVIS: Yeah, it was pretty tight. I remember, as we came in there, of course, there were trees on either side of the road. Coming into the road, we were about a little over 10,000 to 10,500 feet, I think. I remember there being road signs. One was in front of the aircraft and the other one was back off to the side, so the crew was calling that out and making sure we didn't hit any one of those signs as we came down.

MIKE: On a scale from one to ten, one being the easiest, how would you rate that rescue?

TRAVIS: You know, because of the altitude, that's one of the things up here that we deal with a lot. With the altitude is the power requirements on the aircraft and it is a little different from flying up here than it is flying at sea level, so our power margins are not as much.

With all of that, it definitely makes it more difficult, and I would say it was around a six or seven on the scale of difficulty. Just because of those factors and then you throw in the tighter area. I mean it really wasn't, I mean it was confined, we call it a confined area, and you know when you're landing, the width of the road is the same as the width of the helicopter. The trees beyond that being another 20 feet over there makes it kind of tight. It was in a windy part of the road and there was some slope to it and all of that stuff makes it a little more challenging, I guess.

MIKE: I was under the impression that they gave me a 50-50 chance to make the flight to Denver, but I think he was trying to boost my morale. They say that is was really under 10 percent? I really think that most of the responders did not think I would make it to Denver.

TRAVIS: I remember one of the big concerns was, because of exposure and you had been out there so long. Everybody, I think, was thinking that you had been out there for three days or longer. That, I guess, makes everybody believe that you were right at that edge. But, because of the fact you weren't out there that long, not as long as we thought, and I don't know if you ever determined that.

MIKE: Well, it is an interesting question, one that definitely falls into some grey area. Personally, I can't recall other than the fact that my dog had died, and I had a lot on my mind and I am pretty sure I left around dusk. The rescue was on June 9, 2015. The only thing we can go off of is what the surgeon's report. Apparently, my left arm was ripped off and was underneath me. Judging from forensics of something, they came up with 33 hours. Now, I really don't think I was there for that long, but I was probably down there overnight.

TRAVIS: I remember that the bike was on top of you, which, I believe from discussion, actually helped a little bit because it restricted the blood flow, so it didn't allow you to bleed out. I think that, even though it was a bad thing, it was important. I remember you were talking in the aircraft and you were semi-coherent and were beginning to answer questions from the crew. I am sure the crew can speak to that a little bit better.

But, I do remember one part that was pretty vivid and I still kind of picture that in my mind.

You were complaining about your left leg hurting. We were in flight to the hospital at this point, and you were complaining about your leg or foot really hurting, can you do something with that? I remember Aaron getting out of the seat belt and going down to reach where your leg was to try to figure out what was going on or what was causing your pain and your foot was actually all the way back here wrapped behind your leg. It was completely folded back, and so when he lifted up your leg, your foot kind of dangled down like this. That is when I think they knew that it was pretty well amputated at that point, but they didn't realize that it was still attached or whatever because you were attached to the backboard. I don't think that they had gotten that far into the assessment to know what was going on.

I remember him pulling your leg or foot out and kind of

bringing it so it was back in line with your leg, which was probably, I don't know if it helped in your pain, but you stopped complaining about it. But maybe because straightening the muscles and tendons and all that stuff that was still attached maybe was enough to relieve your pain.

All I remember was you had a stump here, around this point. We, typically, as pilots, we don't get to see a lot of that stuff, but that I remembered vividly because we don't get to see that very often. We don't get to see the gory parts of this business, maybe facial injuries and things like that. By the time the patient gets to the helicopter, that's usually all bandaged up, wrapped up and covered. But in this case, we were in such a hurry to get you to the hospital that really had not been done.

If I remember right, your pants were kind of still over that area, so they had not bandaged that up. I think Aaron was a little surprised when he went down there to move your leg and found what he did.

MIKE: (Trying to explain the crash.) Have you ever driven a manual transmission? The term that I am using, and I don't know if it is correct, but I call it "shift lag" or being in neutral for that split second. I was coming up to that corner section, and my bike was laboring in first and second gear. As I was coming into that corner, I shifted into third, which was very deadly. The motorcycle was a BMW with its Boxster engine so when you rode aggressively, the pistons actually helped to keep you glued to the corner.

What happened was, when I shifted into third gear, I let off the throttle. Not only was I in shift lag but the bike's center fusion engine caused the bike to correct itself because the center of gravity had been changed. Basically, I was coming into that corner, I tried to shift and I realized I was not going to make it, and I locked up the brakes and skidded off the edge of this 80-foot cliff. I clipped a 4x4 post with a curve sign on it because there is no guardrail there.

I flew through the air, obviously, hit a tree, it came down. I don't know how all this happened, but I don't know if the motorcycle hit the tree and then the tree fell down. It was a 6- to 8-inch fir tree lying across me. There were also many fairly large saplings that also had gotten entwined. Then the motorcycle came down on top of me. I call it a "German-engineered lawn dart" and it came down on top of all that. Apparently, I was under there and I was all twisted up!

That is, basically, how I was found. I still can't figure out what time it was when I crashed and how long I was there before I was found. I'm pretty sure I crashed at dusk.

I will tell you this: I had faith that I would be rescued.

I wasn't in incredible pain, which is hard to believe. You think you would be down there screaming, but from the second I was there, I started doing the extremity thing. I hope that you've never been in a big accident and that you never will, but you move this foot a little bit, then the knee, and try to move your body parts to get a gauge of how badly I'm hurt. I quickly realized that I was trapped. That was it. I had use of my right arm.

Basically, I was down there and I had my helmet on and I refused to defecate in my pants, which was a huge thing. Some people say when that occurs, clearing the bowels, it is a signal to welcome death. I just hung in there.

When I'd hear a car come up, I'd flip the visor open and

yell as loudly as I could, then flip the visor back down and pass out, fall asleep, or fade in and out of conscience. Again, it is actually hard to pinpoint exactly how long I was down there.

Not saying, I'm a super adventurous guy, but, for example, if I'm going to climb a 14,000-foot mountain, I don't call everybody and his brother to say, "Hey, this is what I'm doing and if I don't call you back a one o'clock, send the cavalry." I'm confident in my abilities, and if I wasn't, I wouldn't be doing these activities. It's just that simple.

TRAVIS: I think we have a lot of that around here. You'd be surprised at how many people go out there and don't say anything to anybody.

MIKE: How long did it take you to get from the crash site to St. Anthony's? What would a flight like that take?

TRAVIS: Usually about 35 or 40 minutes, depending on winds for us. Your flight probably took 40 minutes from there to St. Anthony's.

One good thing about it was it was still in the morning and the temperatures were cool so we did not have to burn off a lot of fuel to land up there. We had enough fuel to fly to St. Anthony's, and that was a good thing because we didn't have to stop for fuel. Sometimes we do, depending on the altitude.

Chapter Nine

Flight Nurse Meg Vito

I am Meg Vito. I've been flying for Reach and have been in the flight industry for a year and a half. I've been a Level 1 trauma ICU nurse for my entire career.

I used to work at the Salida Heart of the Rockies Regional Medical Center ER as a nurse, picking up shifts for about four years. I came to Reach because I moved down to Salida three years ago. I wanted to be in the mountains, and I heard that they were going to put a helicopter here so I figured that is what I will try next. I still work at Denver Medical Center, which is a Level 1 trauma facility in Denver, and I work with Reach full time here in Buena Vista.

We got your call. That was my second scene ever as a brand-new flight nurse.

We were still EagleMed, and that is when we picked you up with Aaron, a flight crew paramedic. We knew you were up high. They told us what your altitude was, and that was the first time I'd ever flown up in that area. I don't think that I'd ever been up Cottonwood Pass.

MIKE: Travis (the helicopter pilot) said it was at 10,500 feet.

MEG: We were doing these huge bank turns up there. I mean, I was hanging on. Then Travis landed us smoothly down on the road. We were right there with Chafee County Fire and you were still down in the ravine.

You weren't even up on the road yet, so we decided we were going to burn some fuel off and stay hot. We did not know how long we were going to be there and Aaron actually got out of the aircraft to go down with search and rescue. He is the one who got an I/O in and put another IV in and just took a quick look at you.

I think he gave you some sodium bicarb because you were down there a little while, and it was to help protect your kidneys from trauma that you experienced.

They pulled you up in the orange bucket and that was the first time I saw you. We got you on the aircraft. You were in so much pain and we didn't know if you had blood pressure. We didn't know if you had any pulses. Your leg was underneath your other leg and it looked like your thigh. I have never seen anything like that and this was the first time I was on a real dramatic scene call. You were in there screaming with pain, and we felt so bad for you, but as soon as you were able to tell us how much you were hurting, we knew that you were "with us."

Your blood pressure was actually high because you were

in so much pain. I remember Aaron thought you might have a collapsed lung because you were having difficulty breathing. We had to keep you flat because we did not know if you had a neck injury.

MIKE: (I show Meg the scar on my back.) I think that was the gas burning through my skin and, apparently, through my ribs and that somehow collapsed my lung. Plus, I had a lacerated kidney.

MEG: Knowing that now, I'm surprised your blood pressure stayed stable. Your vital signs were stable, and that's when Aaron darted your chest. We did a needle decompression on your chest and into your lung to help expand that lung, and that was all done in the aircraft.

Our aircraft looked like *Romper Room* in there. We had everything hanging from the windows. You stayed with us the whole time, and I remember you kept telling us that your leg hurt. We did know that it wasn't there, but it was when Aaron tried to move it and that's when I guessed where your left leg was (folded under left thigh). You are such a trouper, I mean the pain meds we gave you and the fact you stayed with us the whole way.

We got to the ER. Aaron had put a tourniquet around your leg, even though you weren't bleeding. I couldn't put the whole picture together because you were still conscious. You still had stable vital signs and you were a hot mess.

We didn't even know about the burn on your back because you were flat and we did not want to turn you, we just wanted you moving. We wanted to take you to Denver and we knew you had to go to Denver, so I think we went to St. Anthony's. It was only a two-minute difference from there to Denver Health. We got you to the ER, and the whole trauma team was there waiting for our report and they whisked you away.

Again, we knew you were broken, so we didn't want to mess with you too much, but our biggest concern was whether you were bleeding somewhere internally.

Knowing that you had a lacerated kidney, and that is where the major clotting comes from, I'm amazed that you recovered.

PART THREE:
Hospital

Chapter Ten
Medical Reports

Now, we transition from the rescue to putting Humpty Dumpty back together again. At this time, I was in coma when they were trying to address my medical issues. A forensic surgeon at the hospital, in looking at my injuries, estimated I'd been at the scene about 33 hours.

It wasn't until a week after my accident that anyone noticed the gasoline burn on my back. They could smell it, but nobody had thought to turn me over to see where the smell was coming from. It required a skin graft.

As I looked at the medical reports, the real gravity of the situation finally dawned on me. It truly is hard to believe I was able to recover from this accident. Of course, I have some issues to deal with, but, overall, I'm doing fantastic.

Here are some excerpts of the reports. These are graphic in nature, but I feel they are essential to the story.

St. Anthony Hospital

Interval Summary

Date of Admission: 06/09/2015

Date of Consultation: 06/09/2015

Vital Signs: In the trauma room, patient's blood pressure was 100/69, pulse 102. Patient was saturating 98 percent on a nonrebreather face mask.

Assessment: This is a 53-year-old male status post a severe motorcycle accident with:

1. Left lower extremity traumatic amputation of the tibia and fibula. Patient will undergo a below-knee amputation with Dr. D-. Because it has been 36 hours since the patient's initial injury, patient's foot is likely nonviable at this time. The patient has been started on IV Ancef and Gentamicin in the emergency department and will be continued on this going forward. Dr. D- is aware of the patient and agrees with the plan. We also will obtain full-length tibia films to rule out any further injury to the knee or other osseous abnormality.

2. Left humerus fracture dislocation. Patient will likely need to undergo open reduction and internal fixation in the operating room. Dr. D- to review films and dictate finalized treatment plan. The patient will have humerus films taken in the emergency department.

3. L1 and L4 superior endplate fractures. Orthopedic spine team will be consulted for these injuries.

4. Decreased pulses and neurovascularly out left upper extremity and right lower extremity. Will review CTA with the Trauma Service. If there is concern for vascular insufficiency, patient will likely need a vascular consult. Radiology read is still pending.

This patient following surgery will be admitted to the trauma service in the ICU. Patient will definitely need secondary survey as it was difficult to obtain history and physical secondary to the patient's severe pain.

St. Anthony Hospital

Interval Summary

Date of Admission: 06/09/2015

Date of Consultation: 06/17/2015

Physical Examination: On his exam, he is alert, but claiming that he thought he was going to die. He really was not specific as to why he thought this. He was able to follow commands about 50 percent of the time. I could not get any real good exam on either the left arm or the right leg where he is supposed to have weakness. I do not think he was particularly cooperative for the exam. Cranial nerves looked unremarkable. He was moving the right arm OK. The left leg obviously with a below-knee amputation. Toe was downgoing on the right, not applicable on the left. He would not cooperate for a sensory exam, nor would he cooperate for a cerebellar exam.

[*Mike: I was definitely not in my right mind at this time, as will be explained in the next chapter.*]

Impression: Patient with obvious traumatic injuries. At this time, it is not clear what the extent of his injuries will be. It is too early to do an EMG on him. I certainly would recommend that he get a psych consult because he seems to have some delusional beliefs, and this would be helpful for his recovery to be adequately treated for these delusions.

St. Anthony Hospital

Interval Summary

Date of Admission: 06/09/2015

Date of Procedure: 06/19/2015

Procedure Performed:

1. Preparation of recipient site, right back burn, 12 x 13 cm.

2. Split-thickness skin graft, right back burn, 12 x 13 cm.

Clinical Indication: Michael Gallagher ... suffered a full-thickness burn to his right back when he was involved in a motorcycle crash 10 days ago. This was treated conservatively with local wound care; however, it was clear that this would need excision and grafting being a full-thickness wound. I talked to Michael's sister, who is his medical-decision maker given his current mental status, and discussed the risks and benefits and alternatives to the surgery.

She understood the risks of surgery to include, but not limited to, bleeding, infection, damage to nearby structures, loss of the skin graft, scarring, and the need for more surgery. She desired to proceed.

St. Anthony Hospital

Interval Summary

Date of Admission: 06/09/2015

Date of Service: 06/22/2015

History of Present Illness: Mr. Michael Gallagher is a 53-year-old male who suffered a June 9, 2015, motorcycle crash and was down for over 24 hours outside before being brought in.

Issues:

1. Encephalopathy, toxic metabolic exacerbating a premorbid psych disease. He has massively improved on Seroquel 300 b.i.d. We are going to continue that. His home dose was 800 q.h.s. of a longer acting +150 of long-acting p.r.n. Not sure how that last bit worked but I do think that this high dose we have him on is much, much better than our previous lower dosing.

2. Phantom limb pain. He describes it as phantom limb pain and it certainly seems to be. I will add gabapentin. He has some oral and IV narcotics.

3. Dysphagia. Is resolved. He is eating and taking p.o.

4. Healthcare-associated pneumonia. Is resolved.

5. Hypernatremia in the setting of renal failure, is resolved. I will get rid of the D5W.

6. Left pneumothorax is also a resolved issue.

7. Acute renal failure. Much improved. He is down to creatine 1.5. He previously required CRT and then I think 1 or 2 rounds of HD. He will not require that again.

8. Foley. I will discontinue that.

9. Left humerus fracture/dislocation. It is status post close reduction.

10. Left below-knee traumatic amputation. Ortho is following He no longer has a wound VAC to that site. Again, he is having some phantom limb pain.

11. L1-L4 vertebral body fractures. Jewett brace. Spine is following. He has a Jewett brace, I believe, for when he is up above 45 degrees. There is a more explicit note by Spine about his activity.

12. Left upper extremity radial artery injury. Dr. C- has seen and is being followed.

13. Burn injury. June 19, 2015, skin graft to burn on his right upper back. The donor site was the right thigh. There is a wound VAC actually over the skin graft and Plastics says it is doing well.

14. Prophylaxis. He is on subcu heparin.

15. Diet. Is dysphagia 1.

16. He is full code.

Chapter Eleven

Coma: A Season in the Abyss

I have always been naïve about the subject of coma, and I have never talked to anyone who has been in coma. The closest I ever got was a friend in high school, Mark Murphy, who was struck by an automobile that was speeding by a local keg party. I was not there, but I heard he was hit straight-on and rolled over the windshield then back onto the road. Due to his head injuries he lost consciousness and slipped into coma.

I would like to say just a couple of words about Mark Murphy. Even as young as I was, I remembered Mark being a wonderful, super cool guy. His foster brother, Mark Desceaser, or Cease, was my good friend in high school so that's how I knew Mark, or "Murph." He was very good looking and had a beautiful girlfriend. They were the perfect high-school couple. He seemed like he was always in a good mood, always smiling. He had everything going on and was a guy that was really going to make it. Fate has a way of being truly cruel.

When I went to see him, he was in coma and it was a pretty awful sight. They had splints on all his limbs to keep them from curling inward. Mark seemed to me to be in a tranquil state, deep sleep as the respirators kept their pace.

I remember being stunned and silent. Mark was, for all intents and purposes, gone, and he wasn't coming back. I truly hope that he wasn't in the mind frame I was in while I was in coma. To be quite frank, it's horrific to even think that he was. This all leads to that most dreadful decision a parent has to make: Pulling the plug on his life support systems. What an absolute tragedy.

***

After my accident, I can't recall anything past agreeing with paramedic Diana Wacker to remain calm or die at the accident scene, and that was probably a great blessing.

Somewhere down the line, I was placed in drug-induced coma to start the multitude of operations and procedures to keep me alive.

This "ride" was one of the most horrific times in my life.

The hallucinations and delusions were crystal clear to me and will be forever embedded in my mind as real. In the next few pages, I will try to recollect the incredible events that I believed were happening.

My first recollection was everything in my room was always in some stage of construction. Plastic draping, dry wall, plaster, and 80-pound bags of concrete mix everywhere. Construction workers wandering around the medical staff, not even looking busy, just racking up the hours. I had the feeling they were putting me away, far from a traditional ICU.

Everyone seemed to be hustled by Mexican drug cartel-like guys, pushing the staff with constant reminders to go faster. I remember being moved out of ICU and taken to a different part of the hospital campus that was a beautiful home. It was decorated like an old hacienda with period furniture. The first time I entered the room, I was dragged in by two bodyguards who sat me down on a chair. Next thing you know, the big guys left, leaving me to look into the video surveillance camera and wonder what was going on.

After what seemed like forever, a voice came over the stereo system in a heavy Hispanic-gangster way, "Mr. Gallagher, what are you going to do?"

"I need to get my leg fixed," I said.

The guy laughed at me. "Why should I fix your leg when you're already dead and now I own you?"

I raised my voice. "But Tom Bell knows I'm here, and he will find me."

"I've already talked with your friend, Tom Bell. Nice man, we even talked a while about me acquiring some real estate up there in the Buena Vista area. Well, I told him you didn't make it, that you died on the operating table of heart failure. You were trapped under a motorcycle for days and nobody thought you had any chance whatsoever."

After he revealed these details he wouldn't have known unless he spoke to Tom, I knew I was in a very bad predicament. Trapped again! These cartel guys were wicked, and they would do absolutely anything that would make money. To guys like these, life had no meaning. Death had no meaning. It was a profession, and these guys were definitely in the major leagues and batting a thousand.

I remember those two monster guys coming in, picking me up and handcuffing me to a bar stool in the back of a cheesy 1970s-style lounge. Everybody seemed to be playing a weird game show where people would go on stage like the old *Gong Show*.

People were getting pretty drunk and snorting tons of cocaine, but when it seemed like they ran out of contestants, that is when a seriously jacked-up woman stumbled into the table I was at. She looked to be Hispanic, about 40, an ex-porn star who was in a lot, a lot, of movies. She started messing with me. There I was, bandaged up and obviously seriously injured, but this woman was going to strip me down and humiliate me for the show's judges.

When she started to take my clothes off, she was rough with me, and some people started to boo. It didn't faze her. She became more aggressive. The booing grew louder. People yelled for her to stop, but she kept at me.

All at once, I mean in a second, the place went completely silent. Even these women stopped dead in her tracks. Something serious just happened. The party was definitely over. Everybody started to sit up and straighten their clothes. All the party tables were put away superfast. This woman slowly backed away from me and she sat down.

Next thing you know, those two monster guys took off my handcuffs and moved me into the gangsters' main sitting room. As I sat in there, I noticed a beautiful Hispanic femme fatale sitting with a chrome-plated .45 caliber handgun on her lap, staring at me with a sexy smile that showed off her rows of snow-white teeth. As I was sitting there, once again staring at the surveillance camera, the monster bodyguards dragged in the hysterical woman who'd tried to undress me.

She obviously knew something I didn't. As they forced her to a chair with limb restraints, she also faced the surveillance camera. A small muzzle appeared in the wall and started tracking us. Back and forth it went. The woman frantically tried to remove herself from the chair. I was clueless as to what was going on. This muzzle spent minutes going back and forth, sometimes settling on me for a while then panning to her.

The femme fatale slowly walked up to the hysterical woman, and placed the pistol underneath the woman's chin and smiled. "You've been warned before about your slutty behavior, but some people just don't pick up on that subtle hint. Do they?"

The woman then went into hyper-mode trying to release herself, but it was an exercise in futility. This chair had hosted many victims in its long and storied career. Once again, the muzzle traveled around and finally settled on me. The woman stopped thrashing, and stared at me, smiling slightly at what she perceived as a victory in this bizarre game.

All at once, the muzzle pointed at the woman and started to fire machine gun bullets into her! It was ear shattering. Constant firing tore her to shreds. It lasted minutes then stopped, but the whine of the mini-gun continued for hours as the weapon cooled. When it finally stopped, the femme fatale said, "Nice work. You really do act as if you are already dead. The boss, he like that. He like that in you. You're a survivor my, blond friend. He have plan for you, and when that time comes, maybe you wished that you have died today."

With that, she sashayed away, showing off that beautiful body of hers. Unfortunately, we would have a second meeting later.

***

Another vivid scene I recall was being whisked away on a rolling stretcher to another area in the hospital. I remember going through hanging sheets of painter's plastic through partially completed rooms into their imaging area. The MRI machine looked brand new. Its packaging material was thrown all over the place. Once I was partially placed in the MRI tube, when a young male child with no shoes and tattered clothes pushed a generator right next to where I was laying. The problem was they did not have a proper gauge extension wire to run the machine, so they used a beat up old Honda generator as a power source.

I was stuck in the tube half-way while they tried to start the generator, but it wouldn't start. People started yelling at this boy to hurry up. Faster, faster! He desperately pulled the starting rope to get the small engine to fire up. "It's out of gas, puto! Hurry, hurry, get some gas quickly!"

The boy spilled gasoline all over the place including the MRI table on which I was laying. It burned my back, and it was excruciating. I was trapped once again. There was nothing left to do other than ignore the burning pain and try remaining calm. It seemed like a century went by before they finally started the generator. It coughed and wheezed its way to life, finally building enough amperage to run the MRI machine.

An MRI can take a long time to complete. I was in there

fighting off the burning pain through disassociation. Thereafter, I was constantly reminded of the stench of my burning flesh because every time someone came in my room they automatically gagged from it. Perhaps this reflected the real-world situation of staff not yet noticing my back burn.

"Please, can I have some water?" I begged

The orderly, a big guy, said, "No way, can't do it, you'll have to wait another two hours. Plus, I gotta get me a bag of heroin right now!"

He disappeared for long periods of time. Not only was this guy a jerk, but this dude was a junkie as well. Great. This wouldn't be the last time my pleadings for water fell on deaf ears.

I remember medical staff coming up to me with a towel to their noses, telling each other, "This guy isn't going to make it, so we might as well get him ready now while its slow."

They lifted me into a body bag. The big orderly laughed about how much dough he was going to make off me. "He's small, so we can't get much on his skin, but his eyes, liver, heart and kidneys should at least get us something. I can't stand to smell this loser anymore."

He came back with three big bottles of bleach that he started to pour into my body bag. "Take this, loser!"

He zipped up the body bag a little. The room smelled of the bleach eating and burning my skin. "This dude will be ready in an hour. Make the call to the undertaker."

I remembered focusing, building my resolve. I refused to let this jerk succeed in his plot.

A rookie nurse kept running over taking pulse readings and getting frustrated when I wasn't dying.

People told the nurse and orderly the undertaker would arrive in 45 minutes and that I better be ready. The rookie nurse used a large syringe to inject me with something that would kill me.

Time dragged on. She kept taking vitals, expecting my death, but their methods weren't working. After several minutes, she repeated the procedure with the same results. People around her argued about how angry the funeral guys would be when they got there and I wasn't dead.

A Mexican lady screamed at everyone, "This white boy is going to screw everything up! Just shoot him so we can get on with this."

When the funeral guys arrived, they calmly explained it was too late to kill me. "Believe us, when our boss hears about this, he isn't going to like it. You jerks are going to screw this all up, and the boss, well, he doesn't like screw-ups! He won't reprimand you, he'll just kill you."

Everybody panicked about what to do with me.

It had finally dawned upon me what was going on. This cartel was running a building scam operation and trafficking organs. The hospital's construction was never going to be completed; it was about extorting money from the public. I mean who doesn't want a brand new medical facility in their home town? Then, they'd get in patients like me and take our organs.

I recall somehow wandering around the halls of the hospital and running into but the beautiful femme fatale from the execution room. It was raining outside and the water was pouring into the half-completed section of the hospital. This woman never holstered her weapon. It was always out, ready to be fired. She seemed to use it like a teacher uses a pointer. Every now and again, she'd fire double taps past my head to keep my attention. Trust me, this technique was very effective.

She sat down in front of me. "You know that if this gets out, I will deny everything. I'm giving you a second chance because I feel sorry for you for when that tramp messed with you during the boss's favorite game show. I was sent to terminate you because you have become a problem, but I like you for some reason. It's too bad you're a gringo ... I'll tell the boss I felt that you were close to death, so why waste ammunition on somebody who is already dead? Now, get back to the ICU and just shut up! If this gets out, I'll personally skin you alive before dousing you with petrol and lighting your up. Got it?"

"Yeah, I get it," I said.

***

With that behind me, I returned to ICU and saw a new shift of medical staff. As always, they gagged upon entering my room, due to the smell of burning flesh. They decided it would be best to move me to a special room. During the transfer, they talked about how bad I smelled. One nurse said emergency responders told her that burned people just continued to cook internally once in a body bag.

"That's the smell. He's still burning. How do we put him out?"

"That's not our problem. Let's just get him down there and let those guys deal with it."

The special area looked like a triple-axle truck trailer, and I guessed it was the perfect place for me to be as I slowly continued to descend into an abyss that I would not wish on anyone.

I can never forget the layout of this little area. On my left was a big glass window that looked into a courtyard, but all the items in this room were my enemies.

I was determined to not only survive but to mess with anybody who had anything to do with the unethical treatment I was going through.

Behind me was the IV and IO stand that was pouring saline solution into my system. I was so thirsty I tried to get that bag down to drink that cold liquid dangling by my head. In my effort, I created an electrical short that, in turn, mildly electrified the entire bed. The sensation was like putting your tongue on a D-cell battery and getting that weird taste from the terminals, low level but I could feel it coursing through my body. I was so thirsty, but the staff insisted I'd have to wait another hour because those were the doctors' orders. Where were the doctors?

In front of me, a television was showing Scientology infomercials over and over with no sound – but down the hall another television was replaying a Cal-Stanford football game over and over with the volume on full blast.

On the wall was my nemesis, the Big Clock. The battle was based on the time I was going to be ready to die. I had to clean the slate with God, and it should take ten more minutes. At, say, 5:15 p.m. I'd be ready to submit myself to my Higher Power's next level, which I was hoping was heaven but possibly could be hell. That time would pass, but it would all start again. I bargained with God to give me a little more time. At 6:20 p.m. I'd be ready. This would repeat over and over as I stared at the idyllic, silent world of Scientology on the TV.

A crucifix hung over the door. I'd look at it while a nice young woman, dressed in white, brought her portable Yamaha keyboard in my room and played "Danny Boy" for me. As she finished this traditional Irish mourning song, I stared at the crucifix, thinking it was again going to be time for God to decide my fate.

On a table was a computer screen set up by the funeral guys to notify the family by email within seconds of their loved one's passing.

I took exception to the constant beeping and chirping of the life-monitoring machines. It was like sitting in McDonalds with no music, just alarms going non-stop. I played a game with this evil machine, figuring out how to outwit it. I would slow my heart rate to nothing, holding my breath. I knew you can probably go two minutes or so until you run out of air, so I had to deal with the Big Clock to time the beeps as they slowed down. Then I took the monitor off my index finger. This is how I tricked this machine into thinking I went into cardiac arrest. The computer would send its e-mail condolences. Soon, a staff member would zip in to see what was going on, but stop dead in their tracks holding their noses, trying not to get sick to their stomachs. The stench of burning flesh had a great effect on these people I considered my ultimate enemies.

Once I settled into this horrific environment, I started to meet the cast of characters who had the burden of caring for me, or, more accurately – as I believed in my hallucination – not caring for me.

The "skinny doctor" was always running around like a tweaker on methamphetamine. He would charge in and quickly leave because he always forgot his breathing mask. He would come back in and say, "Hello, Mr. Gallagher, how we doing?"

My standard reply was, "Hey, I'm really feeling much better. Can you please take off these heart monitors?"

"Oh, can't do that, Mr. Gallagher. You know this." He was always chasing his tail and in a hurry to get away from me. I formed a true hatred for this man, so one day I grabbed his arm with all my strength, and stared him right in the eye as I pulled him to the bed. He started to scream, "What are you doing to me? Please stop!"

"I have you in a death grip and you're going to hell with me!" I said. He beat me with all he had to get away from my grip. I laughed so hard inside. He could inflict pain, but starts squealing like a little piglet when he receives any.

His supervisor always wore a light-yellow shirt with a powder-blue tie and khaki pants. He would come in, with a towel to his nose, and brief everybody on my current plan. "Who cares about this guy?" he said. "He's been nothing but trouble for all of us. No one is checking up on him so that's the green light we need to do what we have to do." He laughed as he left the room.

My resentment toward him only strengthened my resolve to survive this predicament.

There was a nurse who wore her hair up like Jane Seymour on the TV show *Dr. Quinn, Medicine Woman*. She was extremely beautiful, and she was undeterred by the smell of burning flesh in my room. She'd always put her hand in mine and say, "It's OK, you can let go now. It's OK. We're all going to die sometime, so just let yourself go. It's OK."

I thought she was an angel because she was not abusing me. That was very refreshing. I could relax just a little bit when she was there. I felt like she was somehow protecting me from all this madness by talking me into dying.

Then there was Beth, but I called her "Death." From a conversation I had years ago with an ex-surgeon, I knew that medical facilities back in the day hired marginally impaired personnel do all the nasty, dirty work that other surgeons refused to do: debriding open wounds, dealing with burns.

Beth seemed to have a serious opiate addiction. She slurred her words and constantly nodded off as she gave me sponge baths. She tried hard but was so messed up she would pass out on top of me. I knew this young woman needed help with her addictions, so I always gave her a pass. At least, she was trying to help me, not hurt me.

Unfortunately, there were others who did. A Ukrainian nurse tried to physically ram a tube up my nose. A tough guy Mexican nurse tried to suffocate me with a rag. At that point, I was really good at shutting down my body. After many failed attempts, he gave up, called me a puto pendejo, then spit on me.

I literally fought imagined villains for every second of life while in coma. It wasn't the peaceful sleep I imagined comatose people usually had.

I have no idea how long I was out, but, trust me, it wasn't a second too long, which is why I called this chapter "A Season in the Abyss."

PART FOUR:

Recovery

Chapter Twelve

Mike's Sister, Patricia Naumann

I am Patricia Naumann, and I am sending this to my brother Mike regarding my memories of his motorcycle accident in June 2015.

Tom Bell, Mike's good friend, called me to let me know that Mike was involved in a serious motorcycle accident and he was in intensive care and in a coma. I believe he thought that Mike was going to be OK. I was actually at Atlantic Beach, North Carolina, with the family reunion that we have every year. With only a couple days to get back to Arizona I flew home with Bill, my husband, and, basically, switched out my suitcase. I then got a plane ticket and located a hotel near the hospital, where I planned to stay for a little less than a week. After I straightened everything out at home, I got on the plane to Denver to visit Mike.

I was not quite sure if I could do anything for him. He was in ICU in a coma, but I thought I could just be there for him and it turned out, when I got to the hospital, he actually had been moved out of ICU to the next floor. That was a sign of progress.

Not surprisingly, he looked terrible, but he did recognize me and he was in and out, but he was on a lot of pain medication.

We talked a little bit, but he was very confused and I think that is what happens to the brain because it takes a while to sort things out. He had some hallucinations or his brain was trying to work things out. He told me that they were trying to kill him to harvest his organs and he fought back. I told him that was not going to happen.

He said he was in a body bag, and they were burning him and he was planning on surviving, no matter what. In fact, he said to me that he grabbed the doctor's hand and said I'm going to go to hell with you, or something to that extent.

I listened to him and he didn't argue with me, obviously. I'm sure this paranoia was just the brain trying to sort things out. With everything that had gone on, putting the details together, the fact that it was such a traumatic accident and there were so many things that happened to his body, surgery and pain medications – all of that was a lot for anyone.

The next day he looked noticeably better, but was still in a lot of pain. With Mike still confused but making progress, I just stayed there and hung out, not really doing anything because there was nothing I could do. We started having conversations about the past, and I think that was kind of helpful.

I talked with the nurses and the doctors, trying to get an understanding for what was happening. It was difficult to find what his injuries were, what the plan was. Pretty soon, he was moved to the next floor, which meant he was going to get some therapy, physically as well as cognitively. There was a big problem, though, because he had so much pain in his left arm and right leg, not the leg that had the amputation.

It was very difficult for him to do any kind of therapy.

The mental therapy and the cognitive therapy, you could tell he was struggling with, but he was getting better and I think the biggest thing was the physical therapy. He wasn't able to move part of his right foot and his right arm.

Obviously, his left leg had the amputation, and they had not given him the prosthesis yet. His left shoulder and arm were in terrible shape, and they were swollen and painful, and it turned out that there was a blood clot. Obviously, that was a major problem.

His right leg had to get up and do therapy, and it was pretty much asking for a miracle. I think he had a lot of pain with the skin graft on his back and changing bandages.

At one point, we asked about his wallet. There was a bag of clothing, but was really just his jacket. His jacket absolutely reeked of fuel. The nurses said they would look for the wallet, but it was never found. I don't know what he did with that jacket, but it was terrible.

Anyway, I just spent the time there talking about the past, Mom and Dad plus Mike's many adventures. I thought I knew most of them, but some of them I did not know. It was good he was able to remember. It seemed like a good way to get his brain working on memories. He had many friends stop by, which was a morale booster. Mike is really a wonderful person.

As therapy continued, it seemed like the nurses and doctors were rushing to get him up and moving just to get him out of the hospital.

It's just my perspective, but it was a very segmented process. The surgeons do their thing, and then you go on to the nurses, and then you go on to the rehab people.

Those different people seem never to talk to each other very much, and, in the end, I never met any of his doctors. I did talk with the plastic surgeon and he was probably the best one to communicate with. The other doctors were always unavailable.

His body had a lot of pain, and I finally asked the nurse to find out what was causing it. She asked me if they should do an MRI. I was surprised that they were asking me about it, but that is how they found the blood clot.

I know what it is like spending time in a hospital, and I always like to have a friend or my husband, especially my husband, being there, even if there isn't much conversation. It's just nice to know that somebody from your team is standing there and you can relax. On the days I spent there with Mike, I basically ate at the cafeteria and came back or gave him his privacy when he was doing something.

I was worried when it came time to leave, because Mike would be alone most of the day. I was unable to stay. I hoped everything would be OK. It was pretty surprising to me that they were going to move him to an inpatient rehabilitation facility. Mike clearly required more healing than they had time for at that hospital. On the other hand, the hospital did a fantastic job because they were the ones who put the pieces back together and the surgeons did an amazing job. The nurses in the ICU, I think, overall, they did a good job at the hospital, but it's just always frustrating to deal with hospitals.

I knew it would take a long time for Mike to recover from all the injuries and also for all the big changes to happen in his lifestyle.

Mike was always the athlete, always on the cutting edge of whatever sport he was doing, whether it was windsurfing, snowboarding, he would just go all the time.

With that serious injury and surgery, I think that he is the ultimate survivor. He just survives somehow, mentally does not shut down. He moves forward, he just goes for it.

I didn't call our Aunt Velma, the only one of Mom's sisters left. Initially, I didn't have an idea how things were going to go, so I waited a few days, until a positive report. Naturally, she already had all of us in her church prayers, but she was good to give some extra prayers for Mike and bumped him up on the list. I think that's a great thing.

A little over a year after Mike's accident, I flew to Colorado to visit him, and he looked so good.

He's dealing very well with everything in his new life. Like I said, he is the ultimate survivor. I am very lucky to have my brother Mike in my life, and he really does inspire me.

Chapter Thirteen

Rehab Nurse Margaret Stone

*M*ike's note: News of my transfer to a nursing-rehabilitation facility scared me. I associated nursing homes with death because I'd had family members spend their last days in them. I'd also lived through the years when nursing homes had bad reputations for abusing patients.

I've been seriously scared three times in my life. Once was when I was wind surfing under the Golden Gate Bridge and saw a great white shark under me. Another time was when I was held at gunpoint by a police officer who was having an affair with my girlfriend. The third time was after my motorcycle accident when I was strapped to a gurney and driven to the nursing home for rehabilitation.

The elderly residents sat in wheelchairs in the hallways watching me get rolled past. Still strapped down, I felt like Jack Nicholson in One Flew Over the Cuckoo's Nest. *I didn't know if I'd be able to walk or use my left arm again.*

I was eventually put at ease. The staff and residents were caring and supportive in ways I couldn't have imagined. In six months, I walked out ready to return to an independent life. I also emerged as a supporter of nursing homes. I owe my recovery to Life Care Center of Evergreen.

***

MARGARET STONE: Mike was transferred from the hospital to our rehab center, Life Care Center of Evergreen, which is a skilled nursing facility, where much of the long-term rehab occurs once a person discharges from the short-term acute rehab in the hospital.

We met Mike and worked with him during a very long, trying time in his life. He was not only dealing with all these new physical challenges, but his pain was pretty severe, and he had quite a few pain medications on board.

Mike had major physical complications including a left lower-leg amputation, a left arm that had fairly severe nerve damage, with only some muscles of his shoulder and elbow and finger flexors working.

He had a large wound on his shoulder blade/rib areas, a skin graft on his thigh, and a right leg that had no real movement in the calf/foot/ankle, as well as, a very painful right knee. His right arm, neck/trunk and thighs were fairly strong.

Our rehab goals were to decrease his pain, increase his strength, and improve his ability to move, heal the wound, and progress to gait, if possible.

The initial focus of rehab was trying to get the muscles to work, especially his left shoulder, elbow, wrist and hand, as well the right lower leg/foot/ankle.

We tried electrical stimulation on muscles that would activate, soft tissue massage, stretching, positioning, braces, and other pain treatments. Mike would try to deal with these treatments, but with high pain levels, limiting tolerance to stretching, so his arm and fingers started to get tight quickly.

During all of his basic functional movements, Mike required maximum assistance initially. He used a wheelchair for mobility around the facility.

While standing, Mike needed maximum assistance of two people to get up to stance, and would yell out in pain due to the right knee. His right knee was one of the more painful areas, and limited much of his tolerance to standing.

We thought the motorcycle must have been pressing on this area, as the nerves and muscles below the knee were not working. At that time, he did not have the full story of a tree limb lying on him at the scene of the accident. Mike just kept saying that he had a motorcycle lying on his leg.

We used a standing frame to practice stance, with the right leg standing, and the left knee kneeling on an elevated surface. It was really painful for Mike, but he plowed through it.

Bed mobility was also difficult, and Mike would sometimes get caught in a position and could not roll out of it. He would move from lying in bed to sitting with a great amount of effort and struggle.

Transferring from a bed to a bathroom was an ongoing challenge. Mike sometimes refused to use a slide-board because it was too difficult to handle with only one arm. He always wanted to do things on his own, and persisted constantly with this.

He didn't always want to keep his stump protector on, which protected the end of the stump from getting injured, because it was too hard for him to put on himself. So, he would attempt to transfer from the bed to the wheelchair without the stump protector on, or without any staff assistance. Because of this, Mike had a couple of falls to the floor, and nearly injured his left residual limb. He would make the staff worried about his safety.

When we finally received the prosthetic leg, and an ankle/foot brace to hold his right ankle up during walking, we used a platform walker to enable his left arm to lean on the forearm as there was not enough strength in his forearm and hand muscles to use a regular walker.

Gait training was a challenge. The prosthesis was adjusted for fit, alignment, and improved quality of gait. His right knee pain continued to significantly limit his tolerance of putting weight through the right leg, and he would collapse in pain because of it, and refuse to walk further.

The prosthetic left leg was not as difficult to manage and tolerate as the right leg was. Every day was a challenge. Mike started to take steps, further and further with the walker, and the staff and elderly residents were all cheering him on in the hallways. With time, he finally progressed to walking with a cane. We probably all held our breath that he wouldn't fall.

Physical therapy also included irrigation treatment to heal the wound on his scapular/ribs, and would cause significant pain, requiring pain meds, and then dressing changes by nursing. Mike would say, "Just do it," even though he was gritting his teeth the whole time.

From a rehab standpoint, he was quite a challenge physically, but the real challenge was Mike, the person.

I think, looking back, this was what probably helped save him. He was one tough cookie to work with. He would move aggressively and recklessly, but always trying to just do everything himself.

Mike frustrated easily, and would blame others for whatever was going wrong. His personality was so headstrong. He required significant pain medications to deal, and would often be asleep much of the day following his therapy sessions, probably due to the heavy pain meds.

Mike would not follow the directions of the recommended technique to do things.

He moved very impulsively, and without care for his safety.

At one point, I think we had to have his friend Tom Bell and his wife visit to help us to convince him to be safe and make better decisions.

He would refer to his left arm as his "chicken wing." (It postured with the elbow back and out at his side, and bent, with the forearm/hand hanging because of weakness.)

He would throw his stump socks clear across the room when taking them off of his residual limb.

Mike would question and resist the therapist's recommendations for the quality of movement and gait, or the stretches needed, or the techniques to activate muscles.

He would decline to wear the braces and the splints that would keep his wrist and foot in good alignment. He often pointed out that he did not have the strength to do what we asked of him, and would get frustrated with this.

Many of the staff commented that, even though he was difficult, we all really liked him.

He was always a gentleman with the much older population in the facility. Here he was in a skilled nursing facility, living among elderly residents, struggling with every movement, yet was very thoughtful toward them.

You knew that even though he was such a tough guy and gave us heck, that he was brought up well, had respect for his elders and was a genuinely nice guy. He would take the time to ask about patients, staff, families, etc. The other residents loved him.

I asked a resident's mom to sew a bag for his walker to keep his items in close reach for when he went home. He was gracious to accept this, to keep all of his stuff, phone, etc. handy, even though I'm sure he couldn't imagine his predicament to need a handmade quilted bag for his walker, made by a resident's mom. She tried to make it masculine with animal prints. He was very gracious and appreciated her work and thoughtfulness.

Once he was up and walking, Mike went on an outing with a close friend, but on his return, he was so upset at how difficult it was to walk with the platform walker in a crowded

Starbucks, and was crushed that he lost his balance and fell to the floor in the store, and everybody just stared at him.

Through all of this, what was amazing was that Mike constantly believed he would recover. He worked at it, struggled and he continues to work on things to this day.

He worked through a lot during rehab and had faith that he would improve. He didn't give in to each road block, but pushed through constantly. He had a really tough attitude.

Close to discharge from our facility, we prepared for scenarios. Mike was moving to a home that was in a fairly remote location. We were all so concerned that he would manage getting around the home safely, preparing food, dressing, showers, etc. We would ask him how he was going to manage a fall, open a can of soup, call for assistance, etc. We practiced getting up from the floor and gave him ideas and techniques to use for safety. Keep in mind that his left arm and right lower leg were not working, and he had a new prosthesis on the left lower leg.

He managed so well!

When Mike first visited our facility within that first few months after leaving, he wore large-fitting denim overalls, which was probably the easiest clothing to manage by himself – creative! He walked with a cane without anyone assisting him. We were so impressed.

He reported that he was working on handling daily activities with challenges, and was so grateful for neighbors and friends who would stop by to help him out. He said he didn't know what he would do without them.

He also was so motivated to get his left arm stronger,

and said that he would go to Mount Princeton hot tubs and work on moving his arm in the pool, and was grateful that they would let him do his exercises there.

Mike visited our facility recently, in late summer and fall 2017. He looks absolutely amazing.

He is now thin, handsome, and strong. He is able to wear regular-fitting clothing. His stance is more even and steady, his gait is more normal and he is now able to walk without a cane. He even jogged in place or danced for us to see.

It's also so exciting to see his left arm doing so well. Mike can move almost all of the muscles in his left arm. The nerves regenerated. He still has some tightness in his fingers, and limited ability to open them, but it appears that those muscles that can extend his fingers are working. Yay!

He gives credit to everyone who had a part in saving him. He gives thanks and acknowledges the miracles, by realizing that each person during that initial sighting of him, the rescue, acute evacuation, paramedics, helicopter and pilot, and hospital staff and surgeons were so gifted in their expertise, and arrived at the right moment in time to help save him (as it was meant to be).

It's beautiful to see him humbled by the miracles.

It has been an honor to have worked with Mike and to see his progress continue. We wish him the best always!

Chapter Fourteen

Occupational Therapist
Carol Josich

My name is Carol. I grew up in Colorado and received my occupational therapy degree from Colorado State University. I have worked as an occupational therapist in Colorado for 25 years, including seven years at Life Care Center in Evergreen, where I met Mike.

Knowing Mike's condition when he first arrived at Life Care Center (LCC), I can say it is truly amazing how well he is doing and how much function he has gained. When I initially started working with Mike, he barely had any movement in his left arm, was still healing from his left-leg amputation, and had significant pain in his right leg.

Mike's physical therapist and I quickly started working together on getting Mike up and standing on his right leg. This was important, as this would allow him to eventually be able to walk with a left prosthesis.

As we pushed Mike to stand in a standing frame, he would become very frustrated and angry because of the fact that his right-leg pain was excruciating. He was only able to tolerate standing very briefly. Along with working on the standing, I would work with Mike on the recovery of use of his left arm, which he nicknamed his "chicken wing." His arm had become quite tight in a flexed position, requiring painful and prolonged stretching. This was important to be able to eventually use this arm even if it were just as a functional assist during self-care tasks and tasks he would have to perform to live alone.

It was rewarding to watch Mike move from a high degree of pain, anger, frustration and inability to a level of decreased pain, anger and frustration and increased ability.

Mike had a strong determination to fight through the pain to achieve independence and be able to walk out of LCC. We were fortunate to be able to go from limited tolerance of standing to Mike being able to walk with his new prosthesis, to go from no use of his left arm and poor positioning, to good functional movement at the shoulder and the elbow.

As difficult as it is to learn to dress oneself with the use of only one arm, the added difficulty of pulling on a tight-fitting stump-shrinker over his residual left leg was one of the significant struggles I witnessed Mike work through. Some days he would throw his stump-shrinkers across the room in frustration, wanting to give up, but he would eventually get back at it and work hard to figure out a way to get the job done. He was determined to do things for himself.

As we neared the end of Mike's stay at LCC, we planned a community outing in preparation for his return home. This outing included a trip to Walmart for some shopping and going out to lunch at a restaurant. This trip became a real eye-opener for Mike regarding what he was facing being out on his own compared to the safety and assistance he was receiving at LCC. It can be quite an adjustment going from an assisted environment where you are not worrying about grocery shopping or having to get around in your community to having to face the obstacles to that level of independence.

As we walked into the Walmart, I encouraged Mike to use the motorized cart. This brought tears to Mike's eyes and he walked out of the store. He was able to explain to me that it had just hit him that he was not able to manage walking on his new prosthesis AND use an assistive device AND manage to be able to get the items he needed.

To clarify, Mike was using his one good arm to manage a cane and he did not have enough function in his left arm to pick up items off of the shelves while at the same time still learning to walk with a prosthesis. This was tough! Mike pushed through, braced himself, and did use the cart to get around the store. The restaurant was another hurdle and reality check. Mike was unable to simply walk up to the counter, place his order and carry it off to the table as you and I are able to. He had to depend on my assistance to place and carry his order for him, which was hard on him. Recognizing "accessibility" – where to park, how far the walk is, is there a ramp or only stairs, etc. – was a learning part of this experience.

When I watch Mike walk into our facility on the days he stops by to say hello, it is always such an incredible reminder to me of his condition the first day I met him and, now, how far he has come.

Chapter Fifteen

Certified Prosthetist Orthotist
Matt Wegmann

I am a Certified Prosthetist Orthotist (CPO) with Hanger Clinic at St. Anthony Hospital in Lakewood, Colorado. This location offers me the pleasure of helping people with traumatic limb loss return to the activities they love, and this is how I met Mike Gallagher.

Strangely, I think it was the film *Forrest Gump* that first sparked my interest in prosthetics — seeing Lieutenant Dan raise his pant legs to revel his titanium prostheses seemed intriguing to me as a teenager.

I graduated Macalester College in St. Paul, Minnesota, with a degree in physics and a pre-medicine concentration. It was about the time I became certain that my prospects for medical school weren't good, that I heard about the orthotics and prosthetics (O&P) program at Century College in White Bear Lake, Minnesota. As one of only 13 O&P schools in the country, Century provided me the opportunity to pursue my interests in prosthetics. I spent my first year learning to fabricate prostheses and orthoses, and the following two years learning how to properly fit them.

I began working with Mike at St. Anthony Hospital in the summer of 2015. His below-knee amputation healed rapidly, allowing me to provide a prosthesis early in the rehabilitation process.

Despite the poly-trauma experienced in the accident, he adapted to the prosthesis very quickly. I recall being somewhat surprised by his desire to eventually return to motorcycling. It was from a phone call about two years later that I understood that he had indeed returned to motorcycling — he explained that a minor crash had caused his dirt bike to fall on his prosthetic foot, snapping the carbon fiber strut.

While I can't say I was surprised he broke the foot, I was very surprised to see him walk in on his prosthesis to pick up his replacement foot.

"Mike, I thought you broke the foot?"

"I did but it's a two-hour drive and I drive a manual, so my buddy Tom Bell and I made this."

His friend had contoured two pieces of flat metal bar stock to simulate the carbon fiber strut.

I entered this profession to help people regain their mobility, so it was very gratifying for me to see that the rehabilitation process had worked and Mike was back to the activities he enjoyed prior to the accident. It was also inspiring to see Mike's refusal to be sidelined — even without a functioning prosthesis.

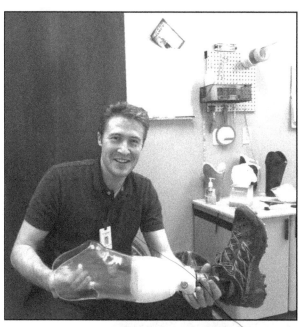

Top: Matt Wegmann made Mike's prosthetic leg.

Above: Mike's friend Tom Bell fashioned a repair when Mike's "foot" broke.

Left: Compare the broken "foot" to the repair.

Chapter Sixteen
Conclusion

The conclusion? I guess the conclusion wouldn't be complete without elaborating on the importance of being a dog owner and the role my dogs have played in my recovery.

As you might recall, the untimely passing of my dog Gertrude sent me into a confusing time, which I believe was a major factor when it came to my accident. Since I moved to the Ranch of the Rockies, in a remote area 24 miles from Buena Vista, I knew that if I didn't get another heartbeat in my house, I was going to be in big trouble. A dog will make you get up and do things.

First, I adopted a black Labrador Retriever mix named June. At the time, I could barely walk, but I had to take care of her and walk her properly. This was a major project and took all my energy at first. I built up my stamina slowly, and if I didn't have June, my recovery would've taken much longer. Unfortunately, I had to put down June only nine months after I got her. Somehow, she contracted a form of paralysis. I could not bear to watch her demise and decided to send her up to that great big river in the sky. I didn't think I'd be so emotionally upset, but I shed some big tears as I took her to be cremated at our local animal shelter.

I was pretty certain that I'd need to transition to another dog very quickly. That is when they came out with Reggie.

I guess, like many of us, Reggie carried some heavy baggage. The shelter said Reggie could be aggressive. Reggie is a Yellow-Boned Coon Hound, and he is from a dog sanctuary in Baton Rouge, Louisiana. It was the site of some major flooding. (When is it not flooding in Louisiana?) He and his dog mates were rescued and eventually relocated throughout North America to no-kill animal shelters.

The only reason I could figure out what breed he was because I watched one of the quintessential dog movies, *Sounder*. It was set in 1933 Louisiana, and follows a young African-American youth and his struggles to find his father, who is in the Louisiana prison system. This young man, armed only with his beloved dog, Sounder, travels throughout old Jim Crow country and takes on all comers when it comes to the vile, derogatory, racist and bigoted South. Sounder was a Red-Boned Coon Hound.

At any rate, after adopting Reggie, I've never seen him show any aggression whatsoever. I know he is gun shy and doesn't like the wiping motion of a fly-fishing rod. It's a miracle he made it out of Louisiana. Other than going missing on a couple occasions, Reggie's been just a wonderful dog.

***

"Time discovers truth." – Seneca

I guess, unfortunately, all of us will become familiar with the Grim Reaper at some point in our lives. I guess you have to challenge him with your overall faith and his plans for you. But, can you accept the path that is laid before you?

I did not think about my life, nor was I reliving my past, waiting for my time to come. I just had faith to keep on fighting and everything would be OK. Coming into the third anniversary of my accident at the time of this writing, spending at least a year and a half doing interviews and transcribing them, I have come to some amazing revelations.

The first revelation: I don't think I was in the ravine overnight as many have thought, including myself.

The accident probably occurred early in the morning, perhaps only a few hours before Dave Bott's discovery.

How did I make this conclusion? Well, in striving for accuracy and a peaceful mind, I figured out that the only real way to establish a timeline was to answer the question, "How long does it take for gasoline saturation to eat through my skin and leave a three-hockey-puck-sized scar and perforate my right lung?"

Once I was in the helicopter, the flight crew compressed my lung in flight. If Dave had found me five minutes later, it would've been a fatal outcome. Because of the tight surroundings and twisted trees and leaking wreckage, the first responders could not roll me to see this unique but possibly mortal wound.

As it was, I was really only minutes from death. For some reason, that really bothers me. You'd expect total jubilation and an "I've got to live every second as it was my last because I'm living on borrowed time!" attitude, but for me, it was daunting and overwhelming. Thank God, time heals most wounds, and time is accruing.

The second revelation: My medal on the motorcycle gas tank helped save me.

Once again, it was a very old medal with the picture of the Sacred Heart of Jesus, and it read, "I will bless everyplace where a picture of my heart shall be exposed and honored."

Because I have 100-percent faith in that badge and its inscription, it's my opinion that the gasoline leaking out of the tank was actually blessed like holy water.

The gasoline initially cauterized my amputated leg and, as horrific as it sounds, kept me warm even though it was on a very destructive path. It also camouflaged the actual wounds, making them appear to be older than they actually were.

I'm sure there are doubters, and that is just fine with me, but this story really happened and nothing in this book is exaggerated.

If this story didn't unfold the way it did, there's no doubt you wouldn't be reading it today. It seems to me that everyone connected with this project has been sent by Heaven, from Dave Bott finding me to Andy Garvey handing me a voice recorder and a pat on the back, saying, "Write your story."

I might, at this time, have some accident-related speed bumps to overcome medically. I am, far and wide, adjusting to the physical injuries just fine. I don't know if I can ever forget the mental damage that was done, but I'm not the only person who has endured a serious accident or major illness.

I think it's a miracle that from the time of my accident to the moment I walked out of the rehabilitation center, with a cane, of course, was less than six months. Unbelievable.

***

My advice to anyone who is injured or knows somebody who is injured: Whatever you do, don't compare yourself to others and their road to recovery.

Even though these words sound scripted, "Everyone has to have time to heal, and healing takes place on its own time." Also, "Gentle words are priceless, but sincere patience without resentment has the biggest windfall to the injured man."

***

In tracking down the people who saved me, I found that my case was one of the most intense they had experienced. Some even quit search and rescue shortly afterward.

I'll never feel like I've fulfilled the debt I owe my rescuers and medical saviors, but everyone I've tracked down knows I appreciate what they did – except for the mystery doctor from Gunnison, whom I never found. After extensive searching, I'd say maybe he wasn't from there.

If you run into a trauma doctor, between 40 and 50 years old, solidly built, curly hair, family man, ex-military, with Colorado connections and memories of working a gnarly motorcycle crash – tell him Mike says thanks.